ORIGAMI 3

Hundreds of thousands of copies have been
sold of the first two Origami books. Here is
another collection of suggestions from Robert
Harbin—the Master of the Art.

There are so many wonderful scenes and
subjects to create—and they're all here in this
the third collection of ORIGAMI, the original
art of paper-folding.

Origami has an appeal which is unique. It is a
talking point, a means of pleasure and a
fascinating hobby using the cheapest of all
materials—a sheet of paper and an imaginative
mind.

'Origami is becoming a pastime for the young
and an intellectual hobby for many adults'

The Times

Also by the same author

ORIGAMI 1
ORIGAMI 2

and available in Coronet Books

Origami 3

The Art of Paper-Folding

Robert Harbin

CORONET BOOKS
Hodder Paperbacks Ltd., London

Dedicated to
Paper-folders young and old
and especially
Danille and Suzan

Printed in Great Britain
for Coronet Books, Hodder Paperbacks Ltd.,
St Paul's House, Warwick Lane, London, E.C.4,
by Richard Clay (The Chaucer Press), Ltd.,
Bungay, Suffolk

ISBN 0 340 16655 X

PREFACE

Origami 3 follows the trail blazed by paperbacks *Origami 1* and *Origami 2*, both bestsellers.

It may be interesting to know that *Origami 1* has been translated into Swedish, Danish, Dutch, German and now French; so wide is the appeal of this fascinating pastime.

At the moment letters come to me at the rate of about two hundred a week from all over the world . . . from Singapore, Malaya, Hong Kong, Australia and New Zealand. So you have friends everywhere.

The British Origami Society goes from strength to strength, and during the illustrating, of this book I have been grateful to the Society Library for the help it has given me.

The Origami Centre in New York is doing a tremendous job collecting, illustrating and cataloguing thousands of folds. These folds, when ready, will be passed to the Cooper Union Museum in New York where they will be available for all to study.

Once again I have tried to fill this little book with more folds than ever before, from as many folders as possible.

Once again there is something for everyone thanks to the generosity of my contributers, whose standards are reaching new heights . . . in fact lots of fine new folds have had to be left out because all the space has been used up.

There is news of a book by the Great Akira Yoshizawa which may soon be available in the English language, so watch out. Always, wherever you go, be on the lookout for books on Origami. They are to be found; I have over two hundred.

Watching Origami on T.V. is fun but sometimes too fast for the slow folder; very frustrating, but books give you all the time in the world to produce fine models.

If you have written to me and I have not answered, I am sorry, it just has not been possible to write to all of you. . . . so keep folding.

Robert Harbin.

CONTENTS

INTRODUCTION TO ORIGAMI 3

My first recollections of paper-folding date from about the year 1910 when children would fold up the edges of a sheet of paper, pinch the corners to form a box and then flatten the edges inward to make a picture frame; or make a paper dart which, rather remarkably, bore a strong resemblance to a supersonic plane. They did not realise, of course, that in doing so they were indulging a desire to practice the art of Origami as the term does not appear to have been in general use in those early days. It did not begin to become more generally known in this country until many years later when folds appeared in the Rupert Annuals and subsequently books by Robert Harbin and Samuel Randlett dealing exclusively with paper-folding introduced the art to a wider public. A rapid increase in the number of people interested in Origami, due mainly to television broadcasts and the publication of the predecessors of this book, has occurred during the last two or three years. The publication of *Origami 3* is an indication that this spread of interest is continuing.

The founder membership of the first British Origami society was received seven years ago only after patient enquiries in many parts of the country. The situation has changed and it is apparent that separate small societies could now be formed in most areas.

This book provides the means of learning essential techniques and of obtaining considerable practice in making basic folds. Full advantage of the experience gained will not be taken, however, unless it is used to create new models. The question is sometimes asked 'What is the best way to set about doing this?' There is no quick answer but we can examine the work of leading folders to learn something of the means by which their success has been achieved. There are many whose work merits careful study. For space reasons only three can be considered here.

Many of Akira Yoshizawa's striking origami creations are animals and birds modelled to most realistic forms. Careful attention is given to details, for example, the shape of a head, the long curved horns of a water buffalo, the hooves of a horse and the webbed feet of a pelican. These models are mostly folded from the traditional Japanese bases which are occasionally adapted to his requirements by being made from a diamond instead of a square. His skills, developed during a lifetime of folding, enable him to model almost any subject, but his portrayal of animals and birds is generally regarded as being the most characteristic of his work.

Eric Kenneway has, for the past year or so, specialised in figure folds and portraits. His approach to Origami is essentially fundamental. He rarely uses traditional bases. The figures, of which he has a fine collection, each one completely different from its fellows, are modelled from a square sheet of paper and are completed with a minimum of simple folds. Full use is made of the colour on the reverse side of the paper to separate hands, faces and the various parts of the clothing. Two recent figures appear in this book. His portraits of famous persons bear a striking resemblance to the original subjects. For these he has devised two special bases, one from a square and the other from a rectangle, from which the models are again completed with a minimum of folds. The characteristic features of the subject are carefully observed, modelled and accentuated, where appropriate, by utilising the contrasting colours of the two sides of the paper.

Neal Elias has made a valuable contribution to the art of Origami by devising new folding techniques and applying them to create 3D models which reach a high level of achievement. His techniques may be broadly described as comprising pleating and box pleating, sometimes combined with established devices such as the windmill and waterbomb bases. Although they are complex they are capable of being varied and adapted to the requirements of each model. Among his many creations are a series of 3D animals, a horse and cart, a waltzing couple and a 3D portrait of Beethoven. He uses paper backed foil, the ideal choice for his very special requirements. It is possible that the work of Neal Elias, together with that of other leading folders, may be featured in a book which Robert Harbin hopes to publish in the future.

From these brief reviews the essential factors of one approach to the creation of original models can be summarised. Continue to study and experiment; start by folding something which has a strong personal appeal but, by degrees, move towards specialisation in a particular field; develop the techniques necessary for the chosen subject; make full use of qualities and colours of the paper; develop an individual style. This is just one approach. Others could be devised to suit individual talents and artistic leanings.

Several references have been made above to paper. A few specialist shops stock a wide range of papers and paper-backed foils of all colours, patterns and textures. Paper-backed foils have the useful property that folds made on them remain more firmly in the position than those made on unbacked papers. This makes them eminently suitable for 3D works. Experienced folders take great care to select the right paper for each model. Akira Yoshizawa chose for some of his models of elephants a paper having a texture resembling the animal's skin and left the folded edges slightly rounded to simulate its toughness and thickness—a fine example of matching paper and technique to the subject. Fred Rohm found for his stag a patterned paper backed foil. The pattern resembled the dappled flanks of the stag and the plain side of the paper was appropriately revealed to suggest the lighter colouring of the chest, neck and head—again expert choice of paper and technique. The study of paper will result in exciting discoveries.

It is a pleasure to introduce *Origami 3*. May it repeat the success of its predecessors and may the series continue.

SIDNEY FRENCH (founder of the British Origami Society)
St. Leonards-on-Sea

The Flapping Bird

An Origami Monthly.
Published by
Jay Marshall,
5082 N. Lincoln Ave.,
Chicago, Illinois 60625.

The Origamian

An Origami Quarterly.
Published by
Lillian Oppenheimer,
The Origami Centre,
71 West Eleventh Street,
New York 2, N.Y., U.S.A.

Suppliers of Origami paper and books:—

John Maxfield,
9 The Broadway,
Mill Hill,
London N.W.7.

The Secretary,
British Origami Society,
193 Abbey Road,
Smethwick, Warley, WORCS.

THE ESSENTIALS OF ORIGAMI

Before you start folding, or trying to fold, any of the models in this book, it would be wise for you to read, and inwardly digest the following observations.

In order to fill this book with as many new folds as possible it has been necessary to economise with the drawings. You will notice at the beginning of many of the models you are referred to folds on other pages . . . this is to save repeating folds which are used more than once.

The Bird Base is used several times. Be careful with this fold if you are not familiar with it. You will see the beginning of the Bird Base in the first column on Page 10. Squash Folds produce the Preliminary Fold. On Page 11 the Petal folding produces half a Bird Base which can be completed by repeating the folds on the other side.

The Bird Base is shown in detail when you try to fold the Turtle. In this case you must not be confused by the inclusion of a 'Blintz' fold, the procedure is just the same with a plain square. When making Pegasus Flying you have a 'Blintz' again, but this time it is on the outside . . . so watch out.

When folding, study the instructions (very few) and look at the symbols and crease marks. Make the necessary starting folds and creases, and look ahead to the next step fold to see just what you should be doing. The step folds are not linked together by numbers, but with various devices, thin lines, thick lines, shadings and arrows and so on.

The connecting devices break the monotony and create patterns which make the 'layout' more interesting.

Some folds are more difficult to illustrate than others. If you have *Origami 2*, you may have despaired of ever being able to make the Jackstone. Page 130 seems to be the stumbling block. You must persevere . . . the information is there, just keep trying. Forget it for a while, wait for a very rainy day and then have another go. It is a great challenge and you will succeed.

Watch out all the time for repeat symbols. These repeat

signs save hundreds of drawings . . . you simply MUST observe them.

Let it be said again and again that Origami is not easy, it is something to be mastered and you must try and try again.

You will probably notice that once again lots of hats have been included. Hats are popular, especially for beginners. Young folders tend to make the first original fold a hat, so lots of hats.

There are many varieties of Origami paper around at the moment. Some good and some not so good. Find a brand you like and stay to it. Good paper should be strong, foldable, and must not 'burst at the seams' when folds are being made.

Several of the models contained herein call for the use of metallic Foils. Sheets of foil can be found almost everywhere. Buy as many sheets as you need and cut them up into the shapes and sizes you need. This cutting must be done with great care in case the result is a disaster. Some folders object to the use of foil as opposed to true paper. Do not let this objection worry you because folds like the Turtle, and the Dancing Lady must be made of foil to get good results. Foil holds its shape better than anything else and of course it looks so rich.

In this book the fair sex have taken charge and have produced some really outstanding originals. Oddly enough there are also some female folds. The Ballerina, the Girl in a Mini and the Dancing Lady. The Girl in a Mini is completed by having her hair and face put in with pen or pencil. This may upset the purists, but there is no reason why it should do as the Japanese have done this a great deal with traditional folds.

You are always asked not to tackle the difficult folds until you have some knowledge of this Art Form. You will only feel frustrated if you do not get results the first time.

Try to find another paper-folder with whom you can exchange ideas, and compare folds . . . form a little group if you can.

A good way to keep folds presentable is to put each flat fold into a little transparent envelope and then to fix the envelope to a page in a scrap book, much as you would postage stamps.

3D models have to be kept in boxes or show cases of some kind. Cardboard boxes with transparent tops are ideal.

If you have been folding for some time and already possess *Origami 1* and *Origami 2* watch out for a few extra arrows in this book. One or two Japanese illustrators use a 'there and back' arrow to show that you are required to fold and unfold, this has been used. Another little Zig Zag arrow has been used to help you understand that a Crimp is required . . . all just to help you a little more.

Finally—take it slowly, fold carefully, neatly and accurately . . . AND START AT THE BEGINNING.

A note on
SYMBOLS

The symbols used in this book are based on Akira Yoshizawa's code of lines and arrows. Symbols must become second nature to you when folding, but you will find that they are easy to remember and apply.

The moment you see a line of dashes, you know that the paper must be Valley Folded along that line. When you see a line made up of dashes and dots, you recognise the sign for making a Mountain Fold. You will then of course turn the paper upside down and make a Valley fold and then turn the paper back to the folding position again.

Arrows show the direction the folds must go. In front, behind, into, under, to this spot or another.

You will notice one arrow used by Yoshizawa which indicates that the drawing has been enlarged for clarity. Another arrow indicates that a model must be opened out for one reason or another. The little wedge-shaped black arrow shows that you are required to sink, push in, press, squeeze or squash at certain points.

The symbols are in fact self-explanatory. They are simple common sense, and can be learnt in about ten minutes.

Try to use symbols only, try to ignore the few words of explanation. Most Japanese books have systems somewhat similar, so you will always be able to discover just what is required of you.

The symbols remember them

Valley fold	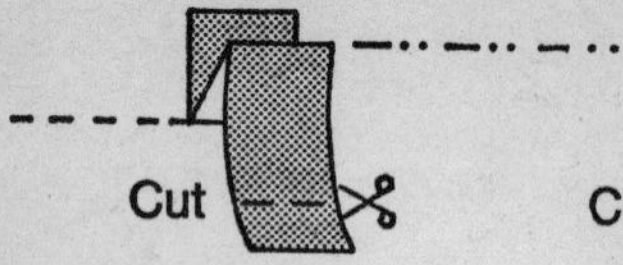	Mountain fold
	Cut	Cut

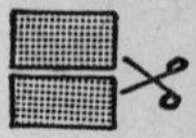

Creases ——— ——— X-Ray view ················

Hold here O Watch this spot X or y

Fold in front ——→ Fold under —→|

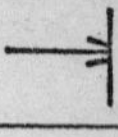

Fold behind

Push in, sink or squash

Open out

Turn over

Fold over and over

Repeat a fold shown here twice —||→

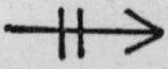

Fold and unfold to crease

8

Procedures   Use of symbols

These symbols denote
a waterbomb base

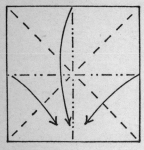

When creased

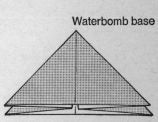

Waterbomb base

This fold results

These symbols denote
a preliminary fold

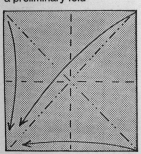

Crease and make the preliminary fold

Turned inside out
these folds produce
each other

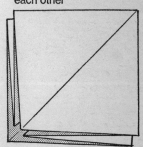

Procedures   Squash Folds 3 types

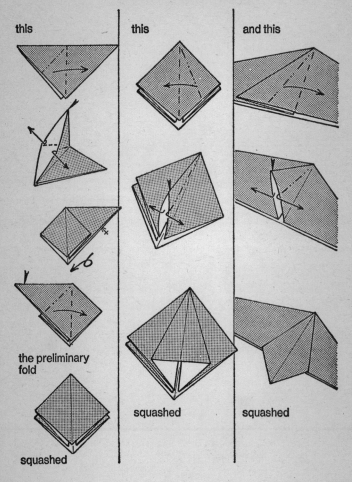

this

this

and this

the preliminary
fold

squashed

squashed

squashed

10

Procedures Petal Folds 3 types

this   this   and this

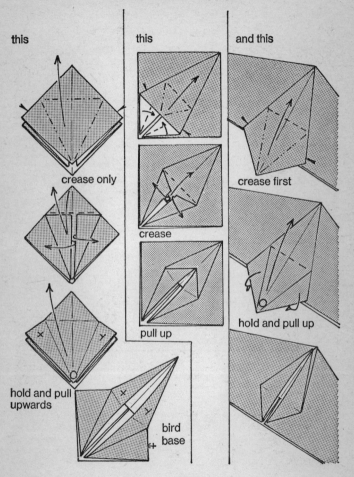

crease only

hold and pull
upwards

crease

pull up

bird
base

crease first

hold and pull up

Procedures Reverse folds

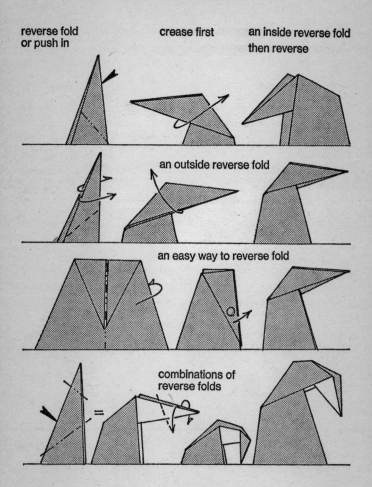

reverse fold
or push in

crease first

an inside reverse fold
then reverse

an outside reverse fold

an easy way to reverse fold

combinations of
reverse folds

Procedures   Rabbits Ears

this fold takes many forms

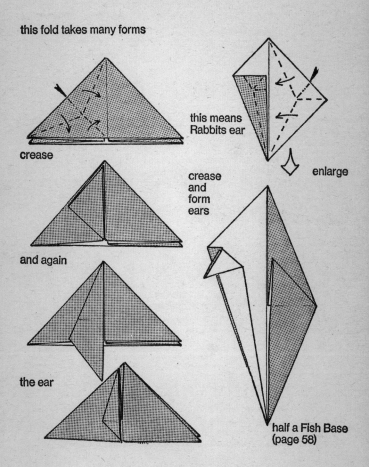

crease

this means
Rabbits ear

enlarge

crease
and
form
ears

and again

the ear

half a Fish Base
(page 58)

13

Procedures Crimps Single and Double

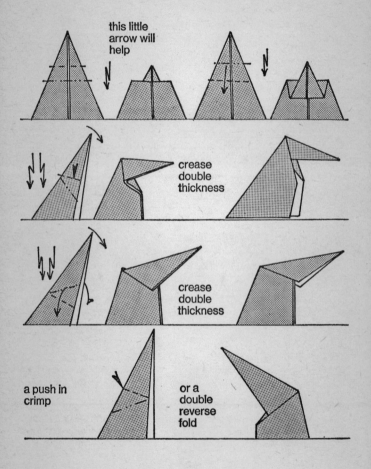

this little
arrow will
help

crease
double
thickness

crease
double
thickness

a push in
crimp

or a
double
reverse
fold

14

Procedures Sinking

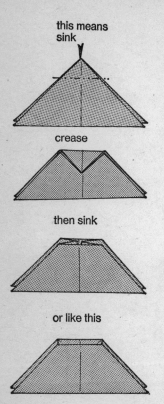

this means sink

crease

then sink

or like this

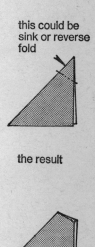

this could be sink or reverse fold

the result

see page 120 for working examples

15

Butterfly

John Smith   England

begin with the
Water Bomb
base(page 9)

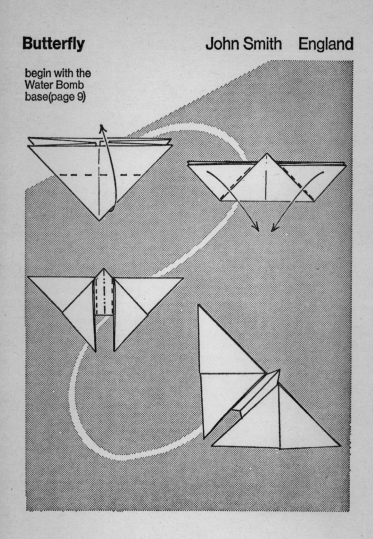

Japanese Man or Genie   David Green Age 12

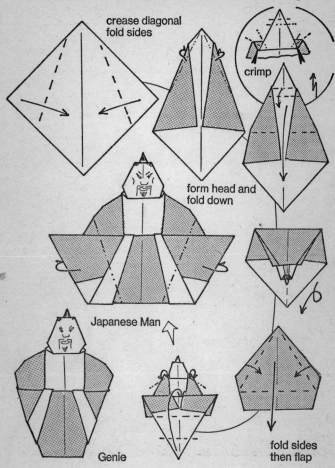

crease diagonal
fold sides

crimp

form head and
fold down

fold sides
then flap

Japanese Man

Genie

17

Easy Box   Lillian Oppenheimer   America

use any rectangle
or square. Try covers
of magazines.

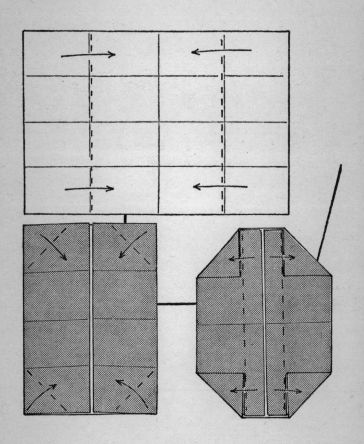

From The Collection at her Origami Centre

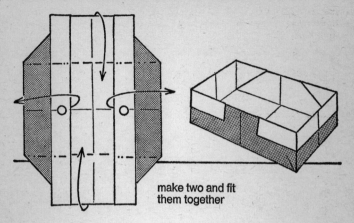

make two and fit
them together

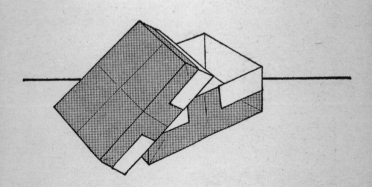

19

Thermometer Paul Powell Age 11 England

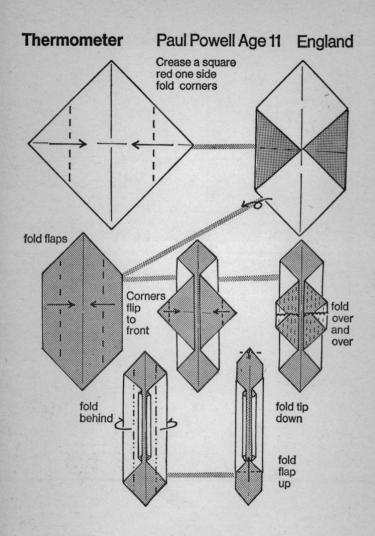

Crease a square
red one side
fold corners

fold flaps

Corners
flip
to
front

fold
over
and
over

fold
behind

fold tip
down

fold
flap
up

Thermometer continued

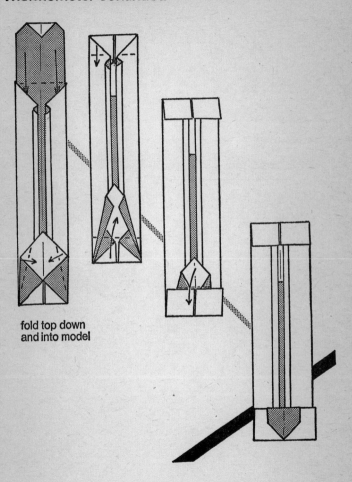

fold top down
and into model

21

Nuns

Vernon Fowler Age 13½   England

Use half a square
black one side

fold flaps
then in half

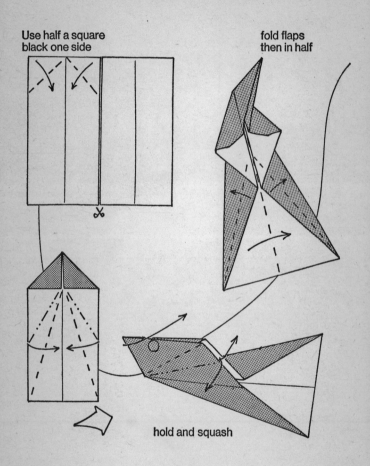

hold and squash

Nuns continued

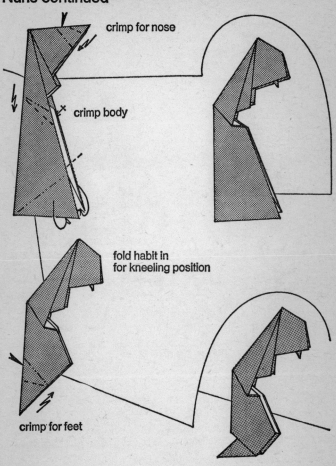

crimp for nose

crimp body

fold habit in
for kneeling position

crimp for feet

23

Grandmama

Gordon Thompson England

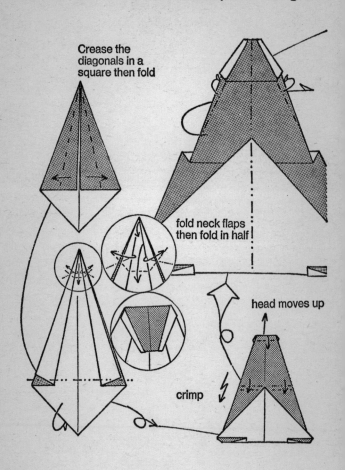

Crease the diagonals in a square then fold

fold neck flaps then fold in half

head moves up

crimp

Grandmama continued

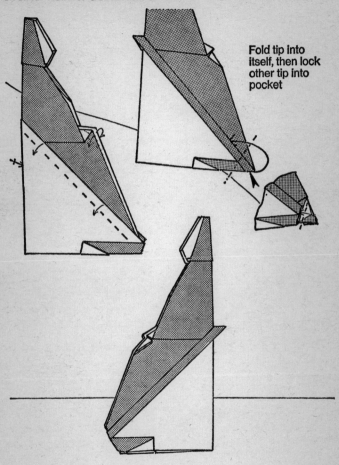

Fold tip into itself, then lock other tip into pocket

Ocean Liner   Lawrence Bisman   New Zealand

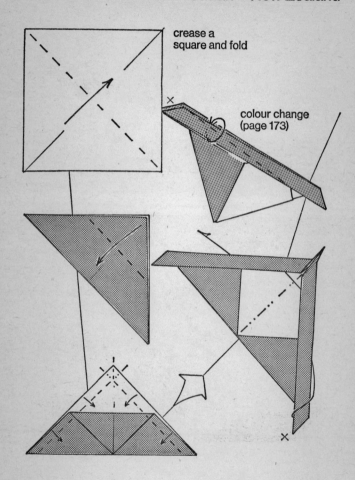

crease a
square and fold

colour change
(page 173)

Ocean Liner continued

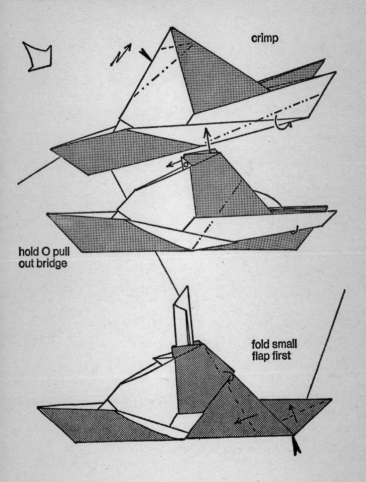

crimp

hold O pull
out bridge

fold small
flap first

27

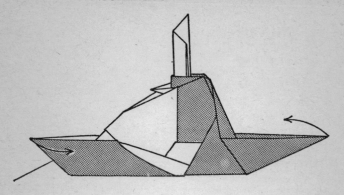

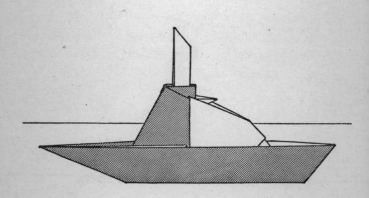

Man in a Dinghy   Robert Harbin   England

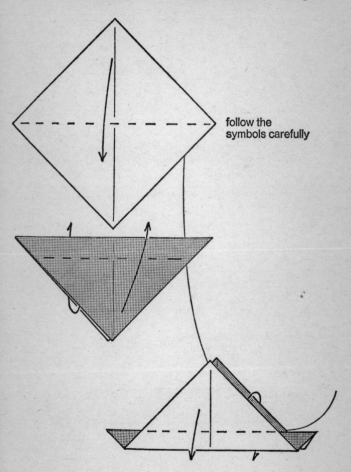

follow the
symbols carefully

Influenced by Neal Elias

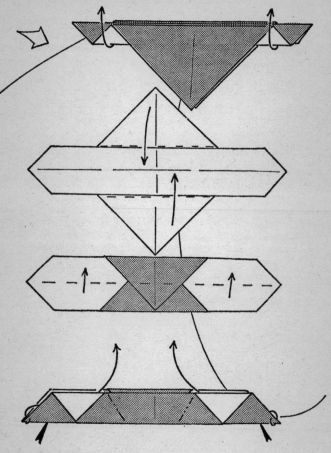

Man in a Dinghy continued

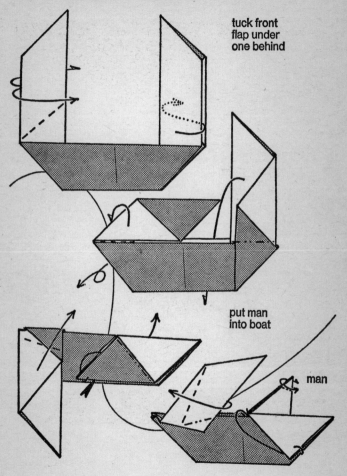

tuck front
flap under
one behind

put man
into boat

man

Man in a Dinghy continued

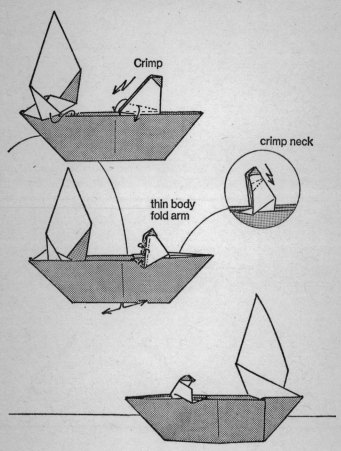

Crimp

crimp neck

thin body
fold arm

Armchair   Peter Wooding Age 14   England

crease a square
fold corners in
known as a Blintz

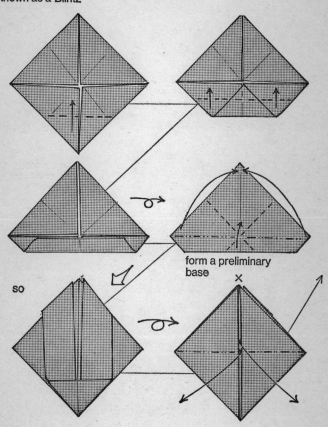

form a preliminary
base

so

Armchair continued

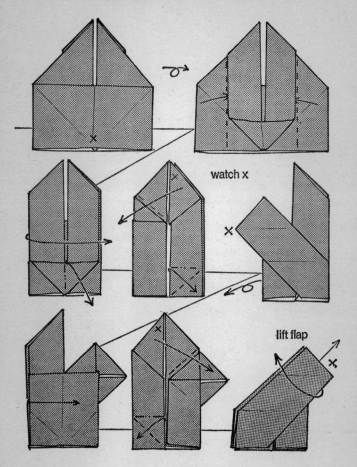

watch x

lift flap

34

Armchair continued

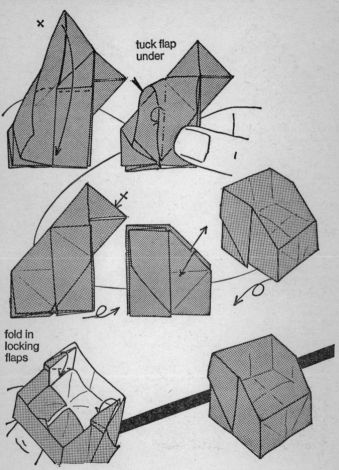

tuck flap under

fold in locking flaps

Hat Variation

Robert Harbin   England

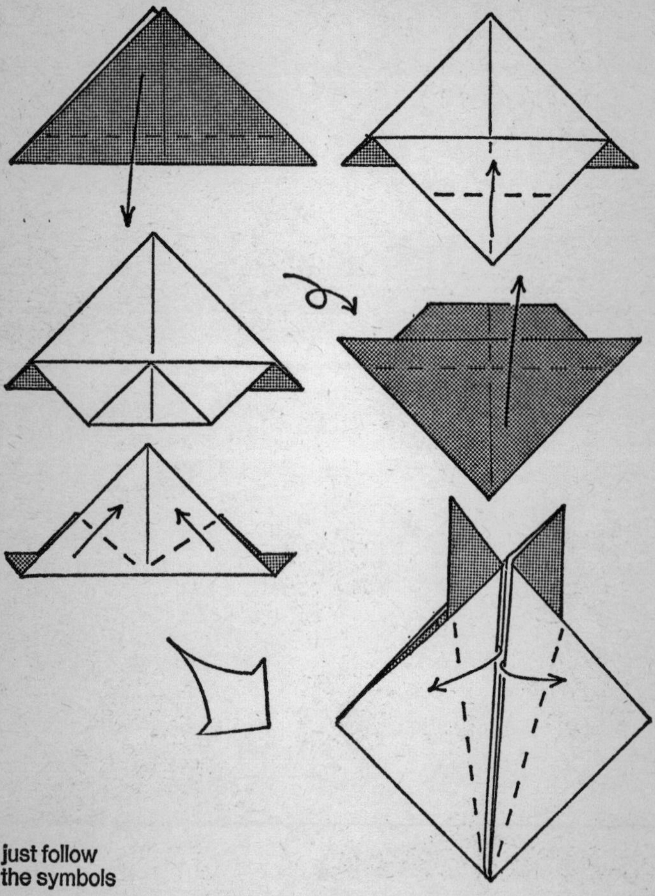

just follow
the symbols

Hat Variation continued

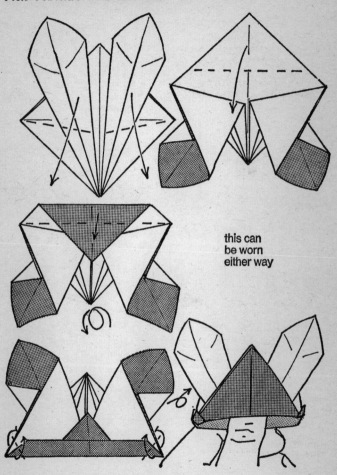

this can
be worn
either way

Box or Plinth Japan

use a 3 x 2 rectangle

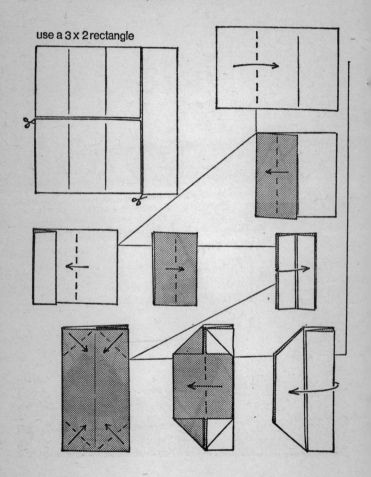

Use 3 Panels from a Travel Brochure

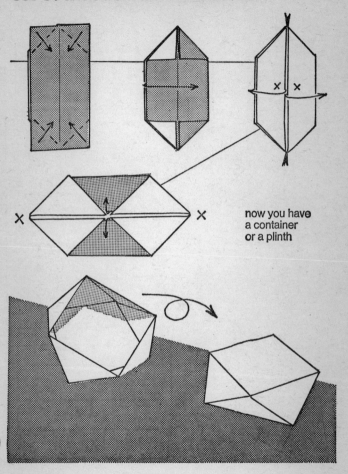

now you have
a container
or a plinth

Santa on His Rounds   Iris Walker   England

use a square Red
one side make
middle crease
then fold

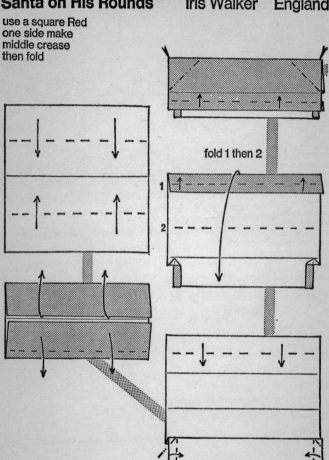

fold 1 then 2

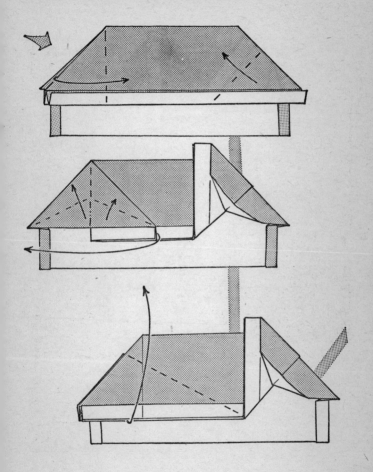

Santa on His Rounds continued

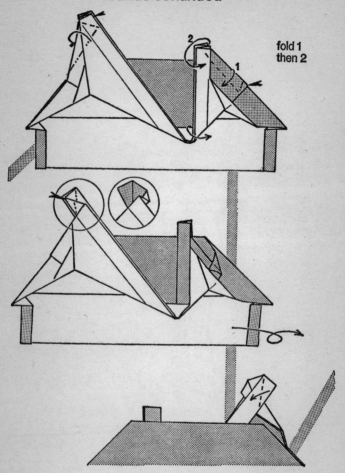

fold 1
then 2

Santa is ideal for a Christmas Card

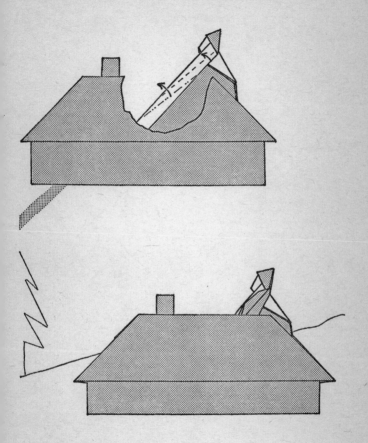

Viking Helmet   Stuart Rose Age 13   England

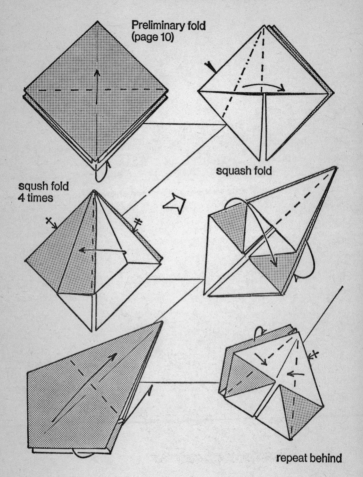

Preliminary fold
(page 10)

squash fold

sqush fold
4 times

squash fold

repeat behind

44

Viking Helmet continued

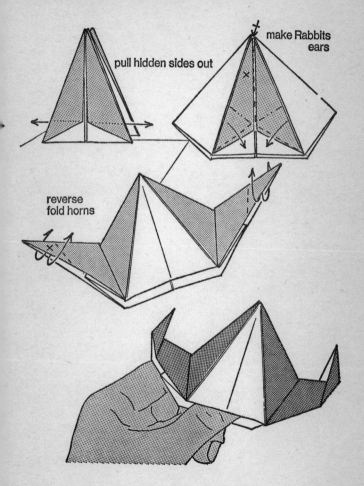

pull hidden sides out

make Rabbits ears

reverse fold horns

45

The Old Man

Eric Kenneway   England

square brown one
side crease diagonals
fold corners and
crease only as
indicated

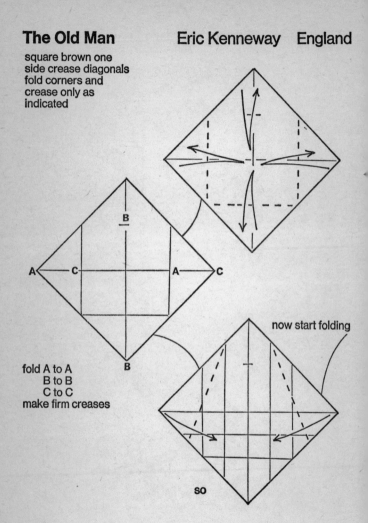

fold A to A
   B to B
   C to C
make firm creases

now start folding

SO

46

The Old Man continued

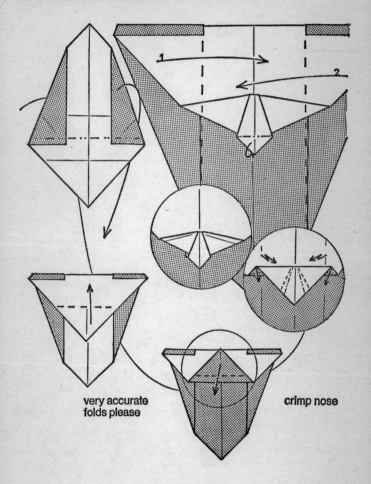

very accurate
folds please

crimp nose

47

The Old Man continued

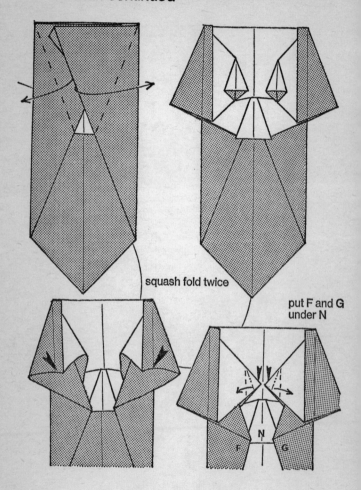

squash fold twice

put F and G under N

N

F   G

Clown

Eric Kenneway   England

start as Old Man
with wider nose

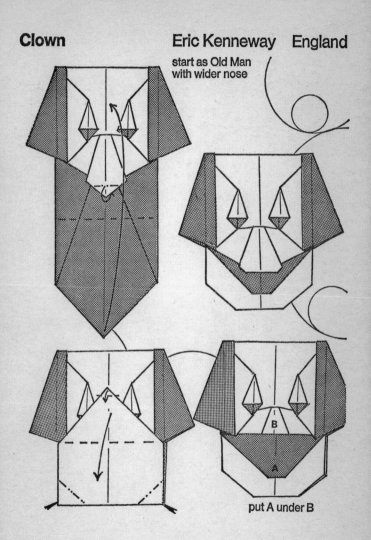

put A under B

49

Windmill

Simon Williams   England

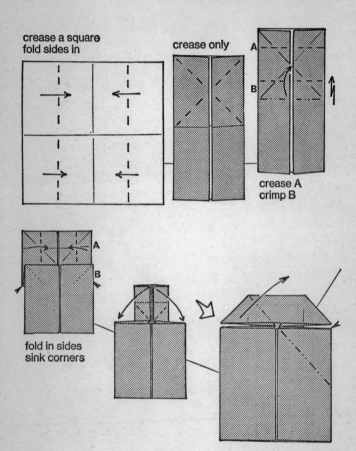

crease a square
fold sides in

crease only

A
B

crease A
crimp B

A
B

fold in sides
sink corners

Windmill continued

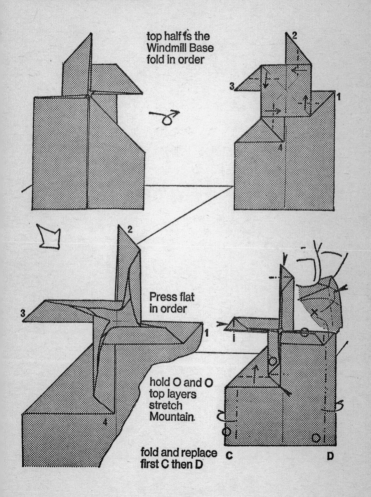

top half is the
Windmill Base
fold in order

Press flat
in order

hold O and O
top layers
stretch
Mountain.

fold and replace
first C then D

C   D

Windmill continued

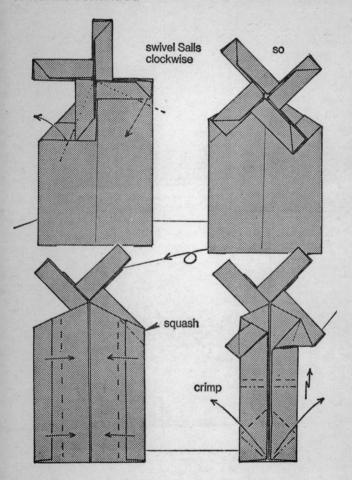

swivel Sails clockwise

so

squash

crimp

Windmill Delightfully different

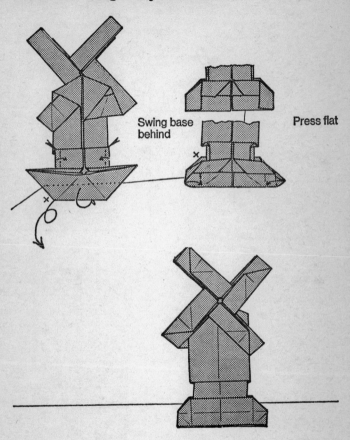

Swing base
behind

Press flat

Windmill Variation Robert Harbin

crease large square
into thirds cut as shown

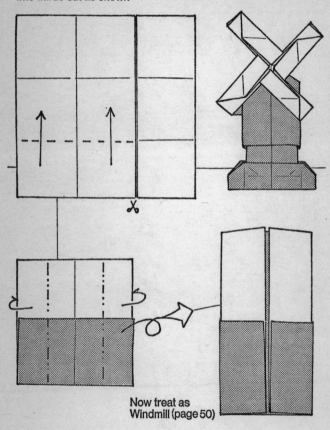

Now treat as
Windmill (page 50)

Catapult Dart

John Smith   England

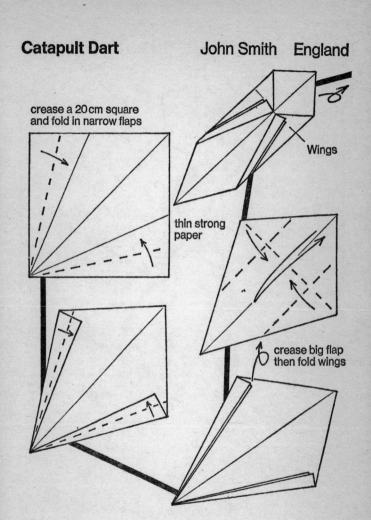

crease a 20 cm square
and fold in narrow flaps

Wings

thin strong
paper

crease big flap
then fold wings

Catapult Dart continued

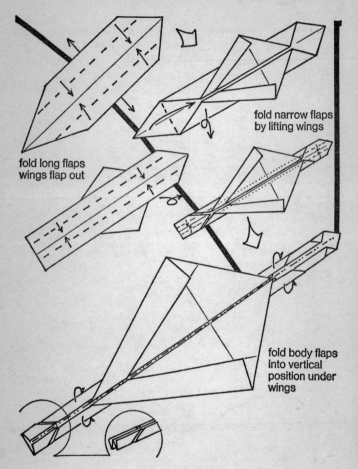

fold long flaps
wings flap out

fold narrow flaps
by lifting wings

fold body flaps
into vertical
position under
wings

The Finest Paper Dart Ever

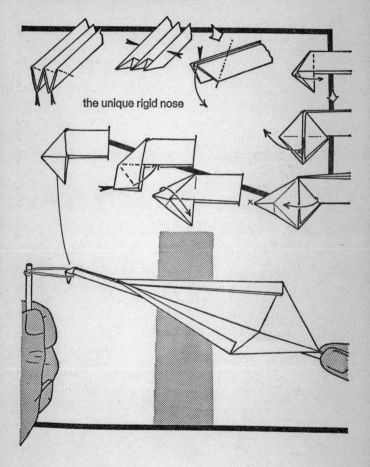

the unique rigid nose

Dolphins   Stephen Cadney Age 12   Solihull

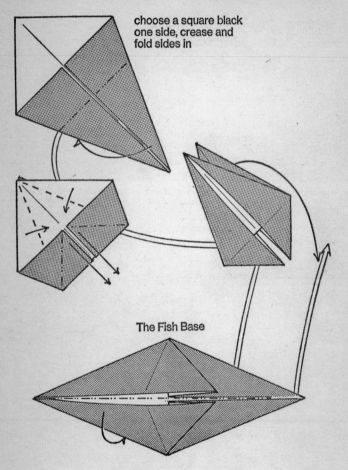

choose a square black
one side, crease and
fold sides in

The Fish Base

first fold a single Dolphin

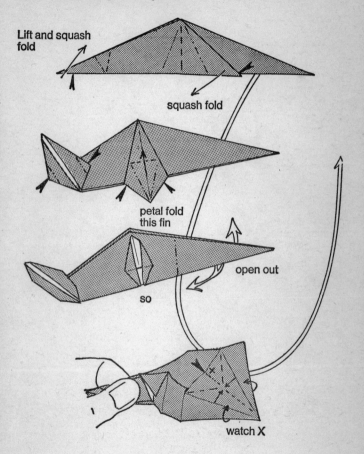

Lift and squash fold

squash fold

petal fold this fin

so

open out

watch **X**

59

now try the double

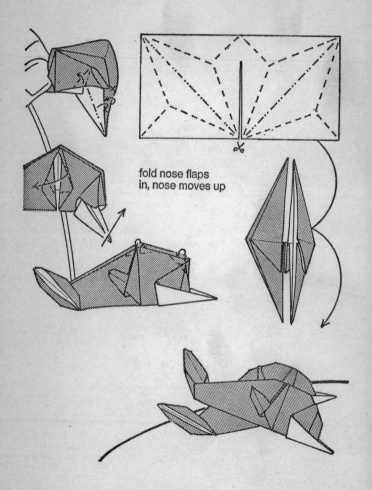

fold nose flaps
in, nose moves up

60

Dunce Cap

Ligia Montoya   Argentina

a large square
makes a Party Hat

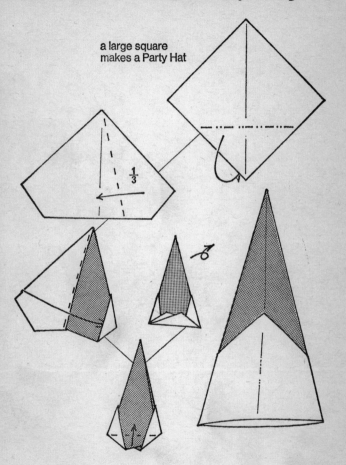

$\frac{1}{3}$

Colonial Magazine Rack Molly Kahn

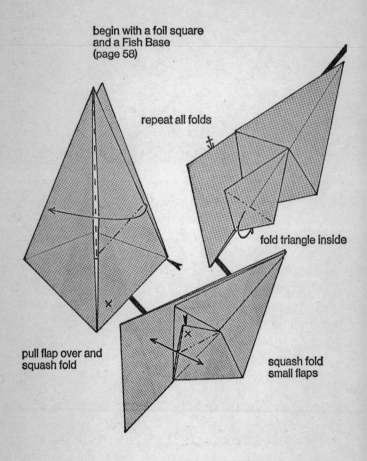

begin with a foil square
and a Fish Base
(page 58)

repeat all folds

fold triangle inside

pull flap over and
squash fold

squash fold
small flaps

Colonial Magazine Rack continued

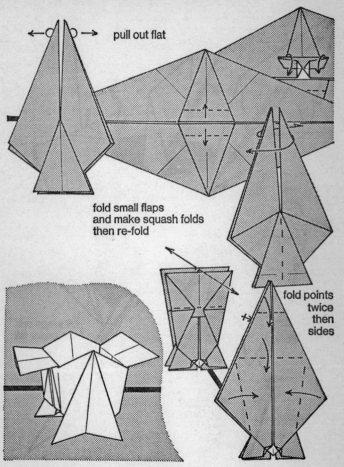

pull out flat

fold small flaps
and make squash folds
then re-fold

fold points
twice
then
sides

Bird Resting

Ligia Montoya   Argentina

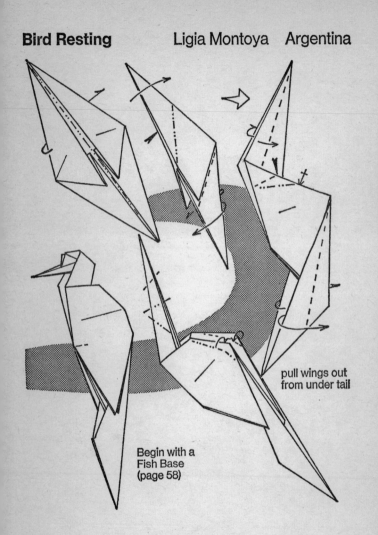

pull wings out
from under tail

Begin with a
Fish Base
(page 58)

Pussy Cat

Toshie Tahahama   Tokyo

start with a
Fish Base
(page 58)

fold points out

press flat

fold in half

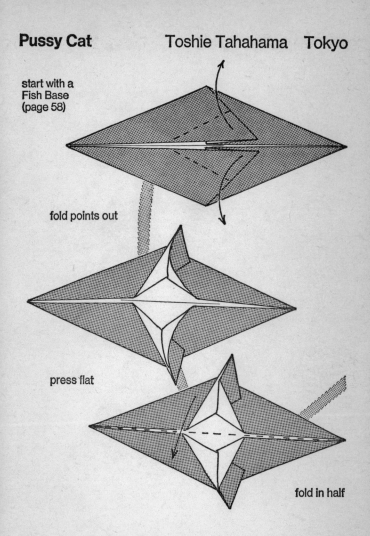

Pussy Cat continued

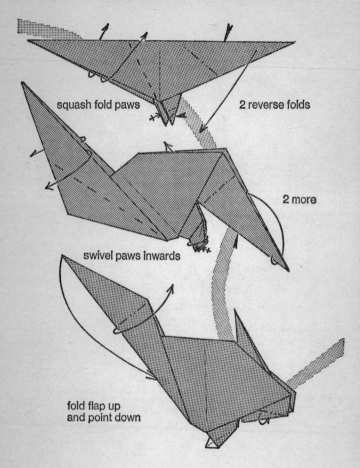

squash fold paws

2 reverse folds

2 more

swivel paws inwards

fold flap up
and point down

Pussy Cat continued

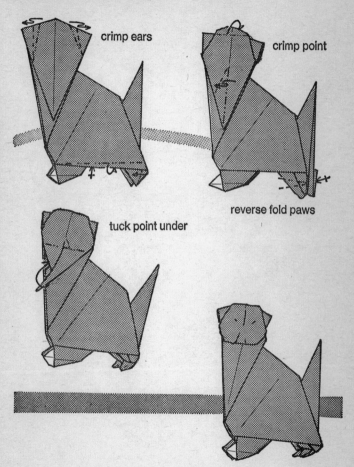

crimp ears

crimp point

reverse fold paws

tuck point under

Jonah and The Whale Neil Elias America

begin with
a Fish Base
(page 58)

sink both sides
(page 15)

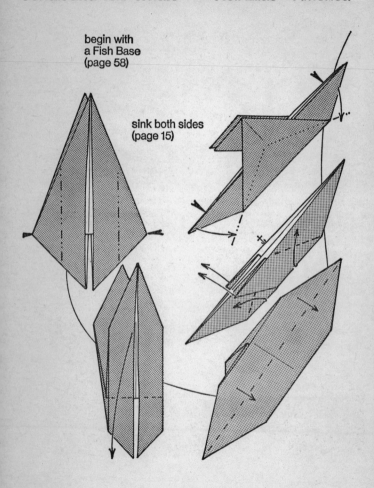

Jonah and The Whale continued

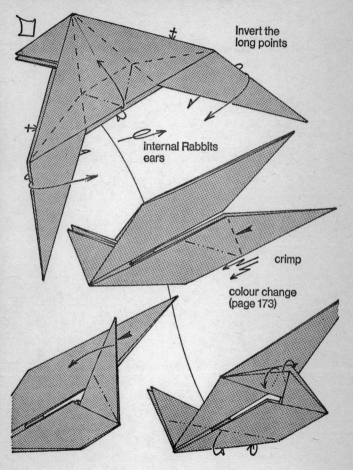

Invert the long points

internal Rabbits ears

crimp

colour change
(page 173)

Jonah and The Whale continued

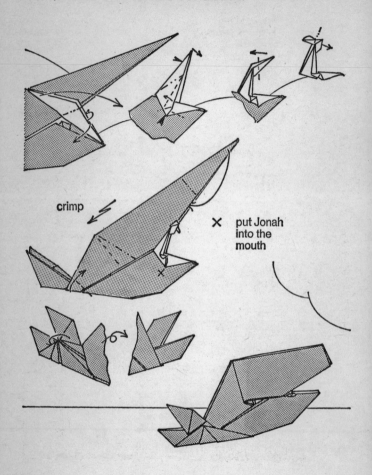

crimp

✕ put Jonah into the mouth

Box

Keith Foster Age 12   England

**begin with a
Water Bomb base
(page 9)**

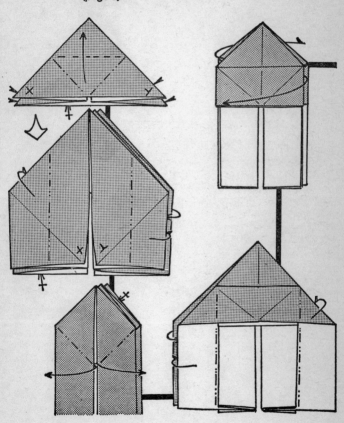

Box and a Tent

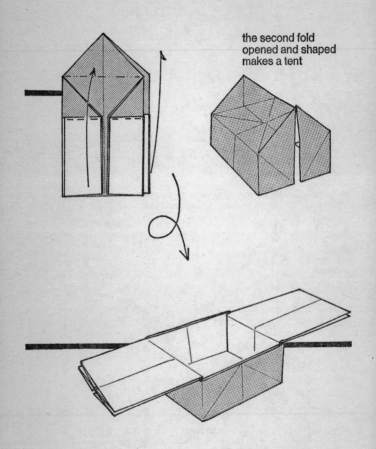

the second fold opened and shaped makes a tent

Angel   Dokuohtei Nakano   Japan

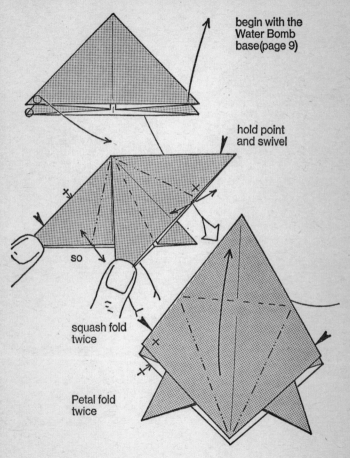

begin with the
Water Bomb
base(page 9)

hold point
and swivel

so

squash fold
twice

Petal fold
twice

Angel Xmas Candle Decoration

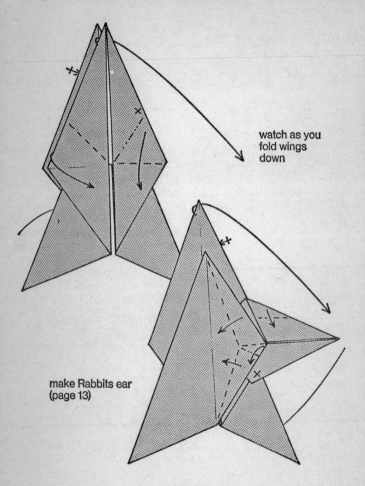

watch as you
fold wings
down

make Rabbits ear
(page 13)

74

Angel continued

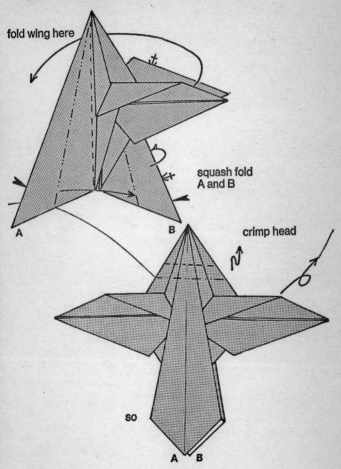

fold wing here

squash fold
A and B

crimp head

A

B

so

A B

Angel continued

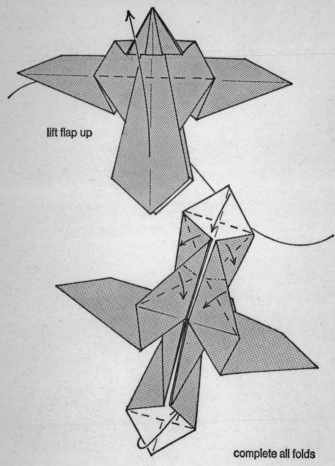

lift flap up

complete all folds

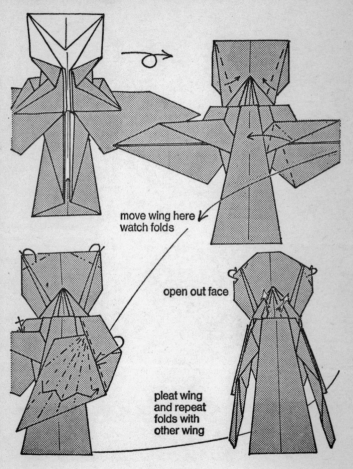

move wing here
watch folds

open out face

pleat wing
and repeat
folds with
other wing

Angel use Tweezers for Face

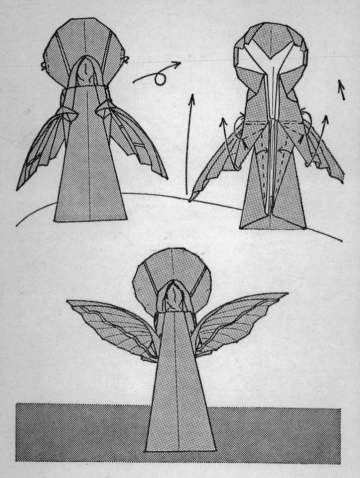

Boat with Sail   Pat Crawford   America

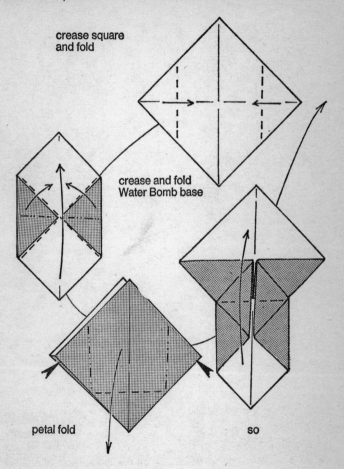

crease square
and fold

crease and fold
Water Bomb base

petal fold

so

79

Boat with Sail continued

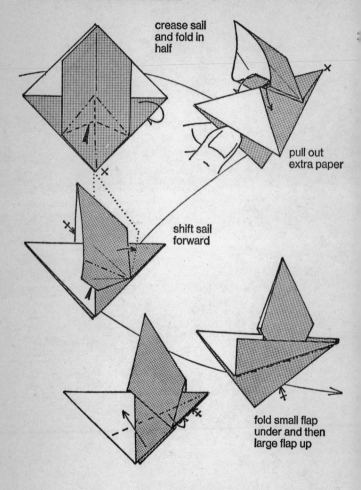

crease sail
and fold in
half

pull out
extra paper

shift sail
forward

fold small flap
under and then
large flap up

Boat with Sail continued

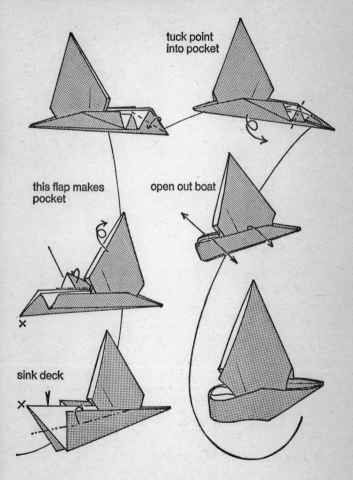

tuck point
into pocket

this flap makes
pocket

open out boat

sink deck

Picture Frame

Robert Harbin   England

use any long strip
of attractive paper

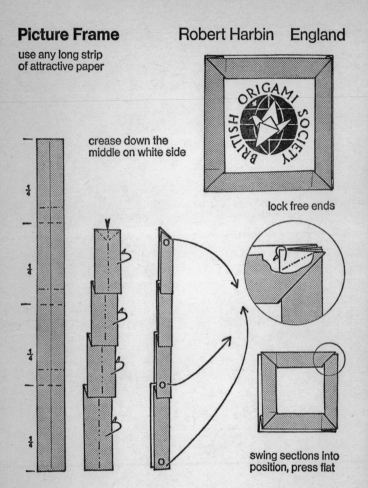

crease down the
middle on white side

lock free ends

swing sections into
position, press flat

Swan

Pat Crawford   America

use a thin white
square, crease
and fold in 3
corners

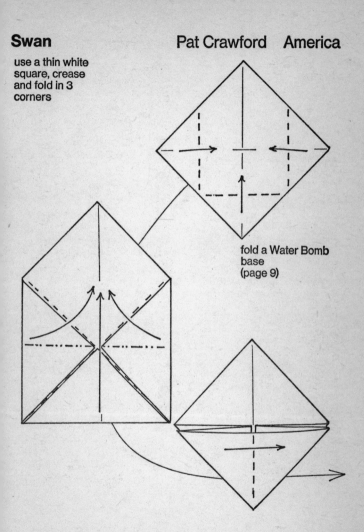

fold a Water Bomb
base
(page 9)

83

Swan continued

squash folds
(page 10)

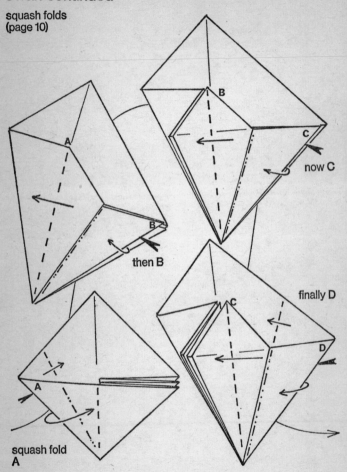

A

then B

B

now C

C

finally D

D

squash fold
A

Swan continued

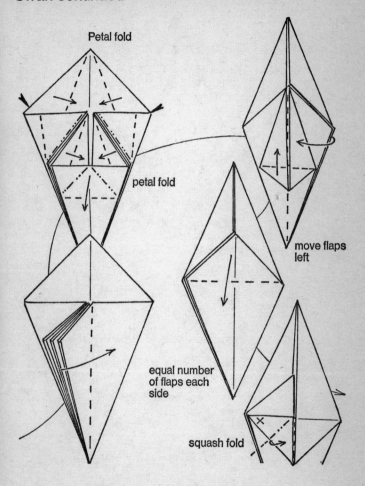

Petal fold

petal fold

move flaps left

equal number of flaps each side

squash fold

Swan continued

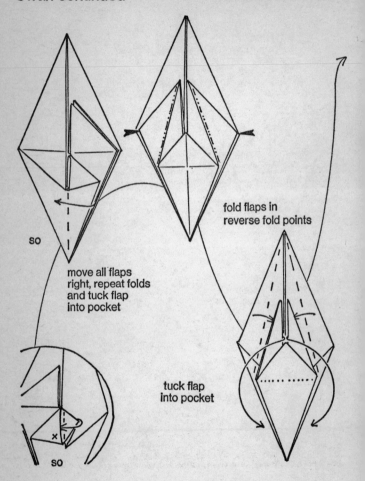

so

move all flaps
right, repeat folds
and tuck flap
into pocket

fold flaps in
reverse fold points

tuck flap
into pocket

so

A Beautiful 3D Swan

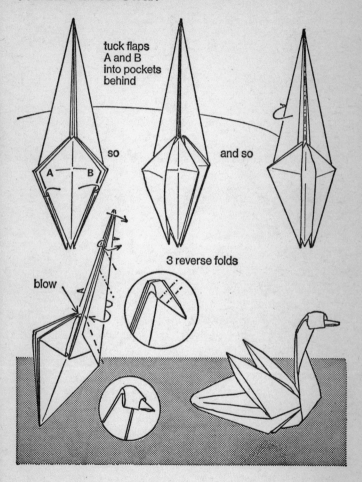

tuck flaps
A and B
into pockets
behind

A   B

so   and so

3 reverse folds

blow

87

Beagle

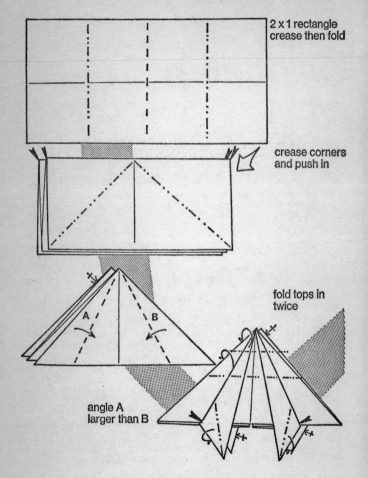

2 x 1 rectangle
crease then fold

crease corners
and push in

fold tops in
twice

A   B

angle A
larger than B

88

Beagle continued

double water bomb base

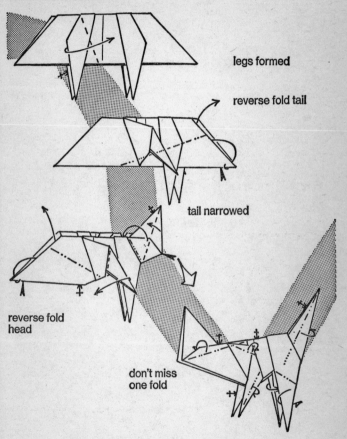

legs formed

reverse fold tail

tail narrowed

reverse fold
head

don't miss
one fold

89

Beagle Outstanding

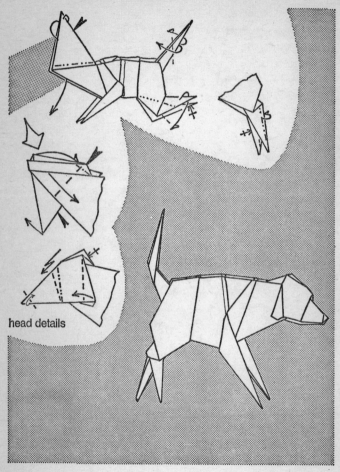

head details

Bowl

Florence Temko   America

square,
begin with a preliminary
fold
(page 9)

fold corners in
and refold. Frog base

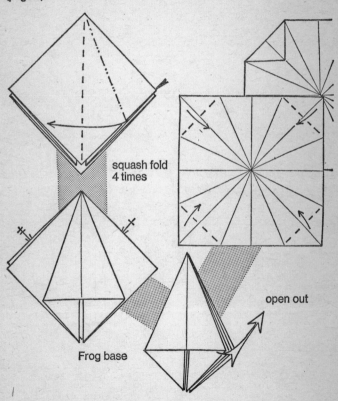

squash fold
4 times

Frog base

open out

Bowl continued

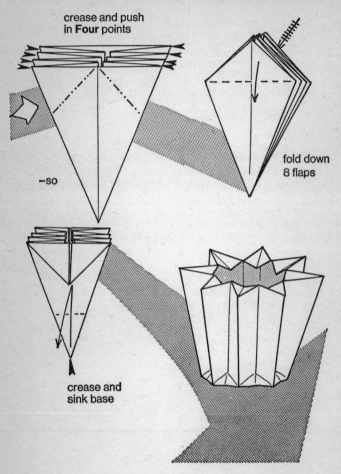

crease and push
in **Four** points

—so

fold down
8 flaps

crease and
sink base

92

Fuzz

Stephen Carter   England

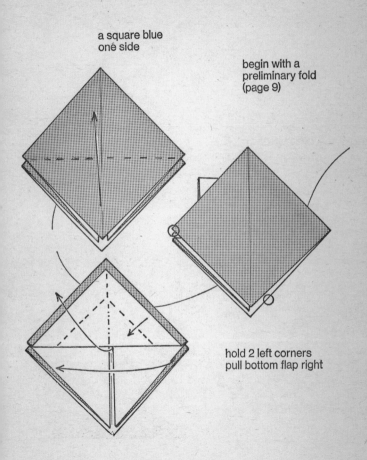

a square blue
one side

begin with a
preliminary fold
(page 9)

hold 2 left corners
pull bottom flap right

93

Eric Kenneway   Portrait Base used

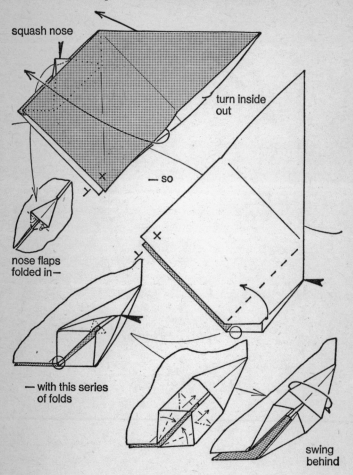

squash nose

turn inside out

— so

nose flaps folded in—

— with this series of folds

swing behind

Fuzz continued

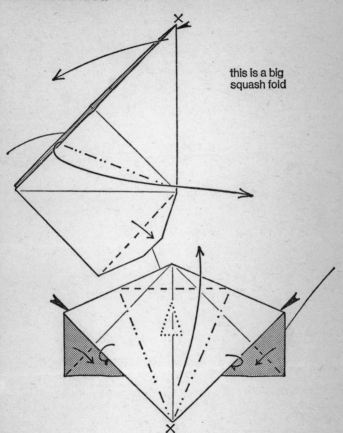

this is a big
squash fold

Petal fold and 2 Rabbits ears

Fuzz continued

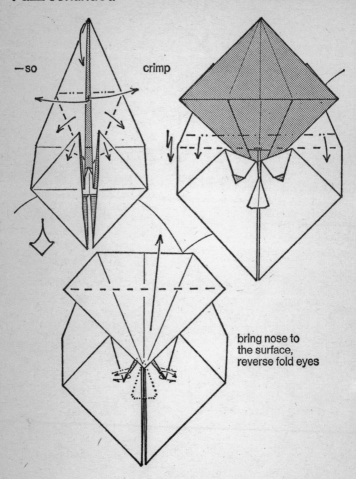

—so

crimp

bring nose to
the surface,
reverse fold eyes

96

Our Policemen are Wonderful

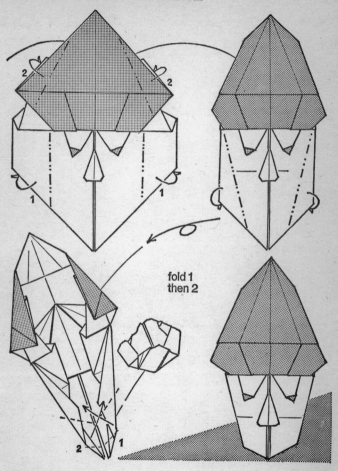

fold 1
then 2

Dougal

Stephen Carter   England

crease diagonals
fold corners in

crease then push
in corners

crease pull flap
left, fold nose
(see page 94)

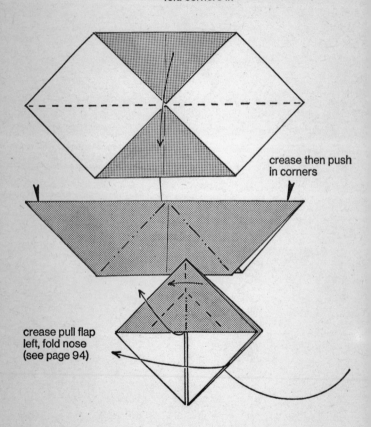

The B.B.C. TV Cartoon Dog

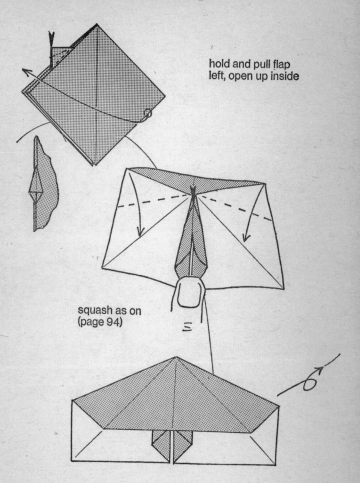

hold and pull flap
left, open up inside

squash as on
(page 94)

Dougal Delightful

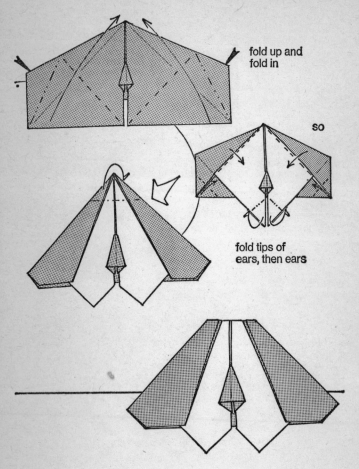

fold up and
fold in

so

fold tips of
ears, then ears

100

Ballerina

Alice Gray   America

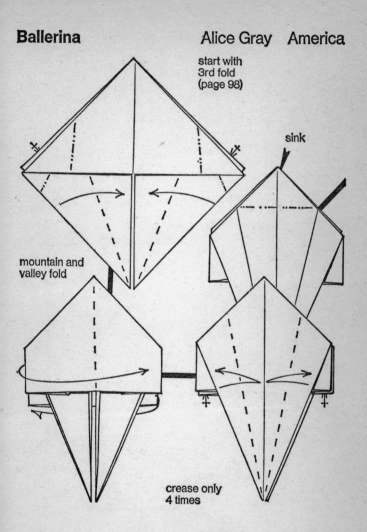

start with
3rd fold
(page 98)

sink

mountain and
valley fold

crease only
4 times

101

Ballerina Legs

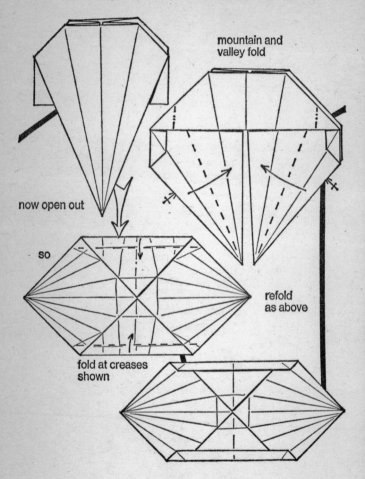

mountain and valley fold

now open out

so

refold as above

fold at creases shown

Ballerina Legs

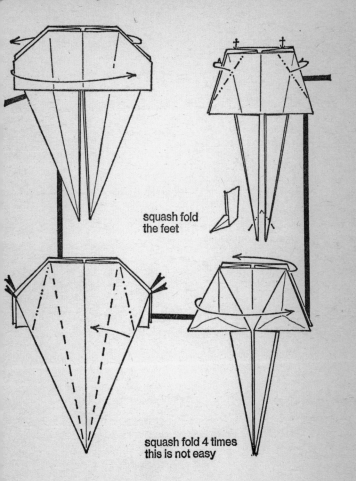

squash fold
the feet

squash fold 4 times
this is not easy

Ballerina continued

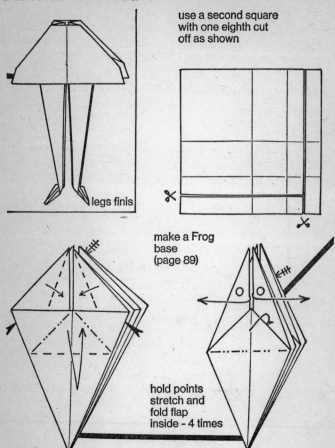

legs finis

use a second square
with one eighth cut
off as shown

make a Frog
base
(page 89)

hold points
stretch and
fold flap
inside - 4 times

104

Ballerina continued

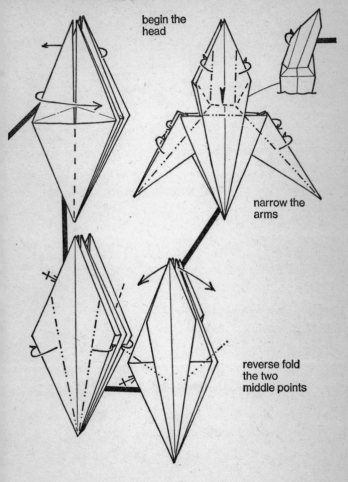

begin the head

narrow the arms

reverse fold the two middle points

Finally assemble the Ballerina

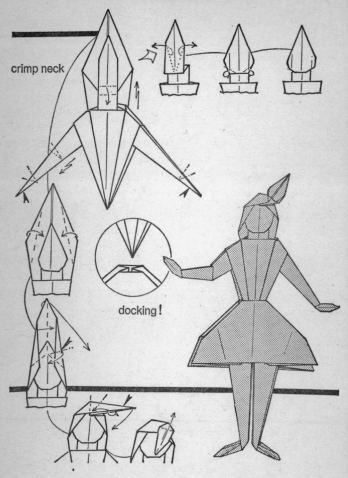

crimp neck

docking !

Goose in Flight

Samuel Randlett America

fold a square
across its diagonal

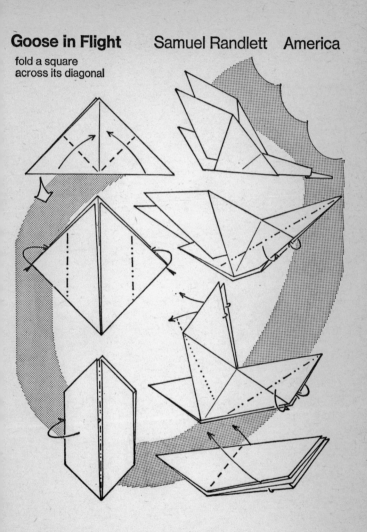

Valentine

Pat Crawford   America

use a square of foil,
begin with the
Preliminary base
(page 9)

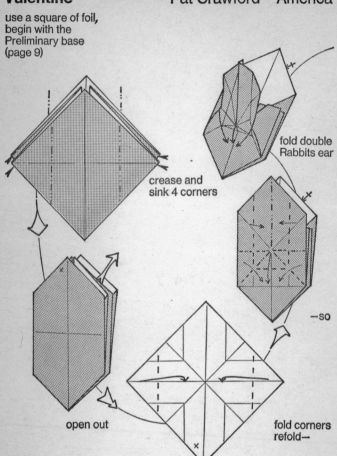

crease and
sink 4 corners

fold double
Rabbits ear

—so

open out

fold corners
refold—

Valentine continued

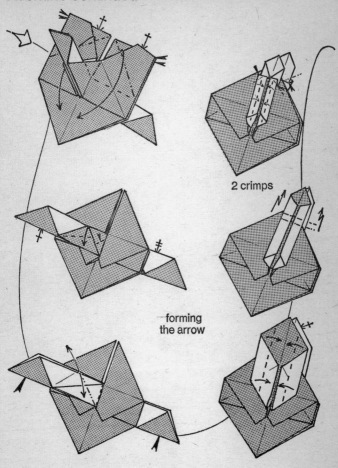

2 crimps

forming
the arrow

Valentine continued So clever

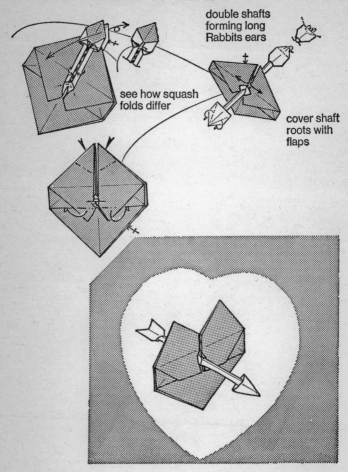

double shafts
forming long
Rabbits ears

see how squash
folds differ

cover shaft
roots with
flaps

Star Hat   Clive Monhley Age 13   England

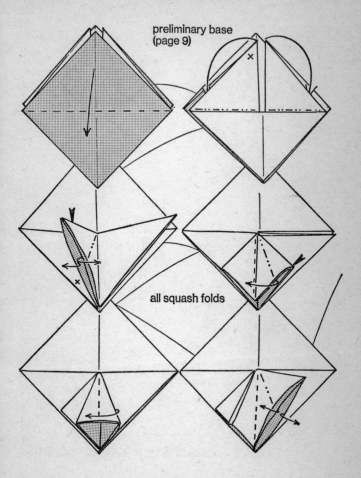

preliminary base
(page 9)

all squash folds

Star Hat continued

shift points
as shown

Star Hat continued

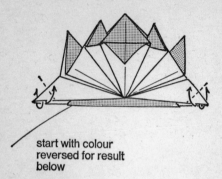

start with colour
reversed for result
below

Pot

Toshie Tahahama   Japan

preliminary base
(page 9)

This is a fine Model

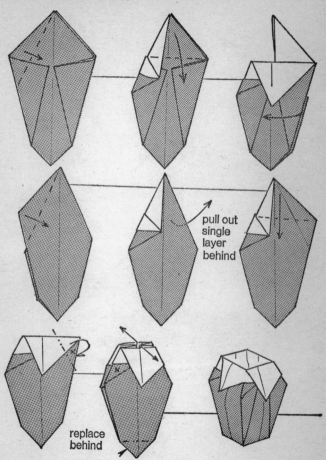

pull out
single
layer
behind

replace
behind

115

Knight on a Horse

Philip Noble   Scotland

square of foil
preliminary base
(page 9)

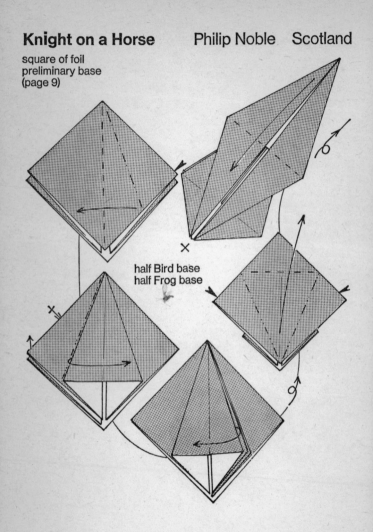

half Bird base
half Frog base

Knight on a Horse continued

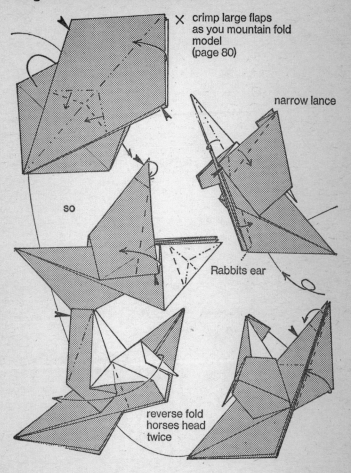

× crimp large flaps
as you mountain fold
model
(page 80)

narrow lance

so

Rabbits ear

reverse fold
horses head
twice

Knight on a Horse continued

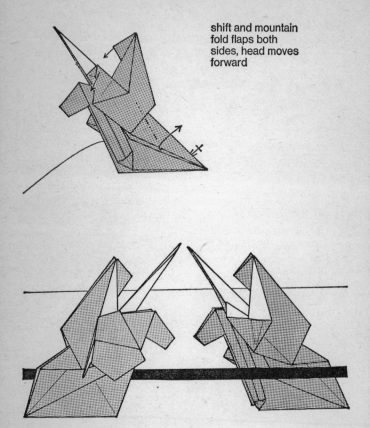

shift and mountain fold flaps both sides, head moves forward

Elephant

Philip Noble   Scotland

begin with a
preliminary base
(page 9)

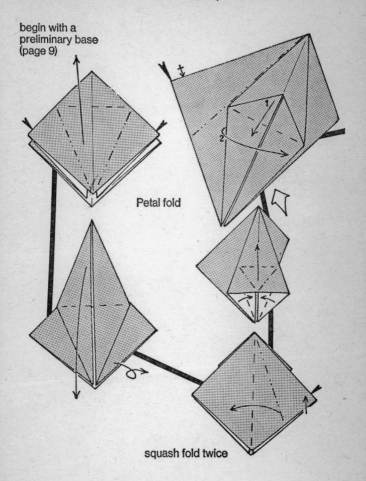

Petal fold

squash fold twice

Elephant continued

sink

sink 2 sides
in the same way

half frog base
half bird base

like this

and this

Elephant   Great!

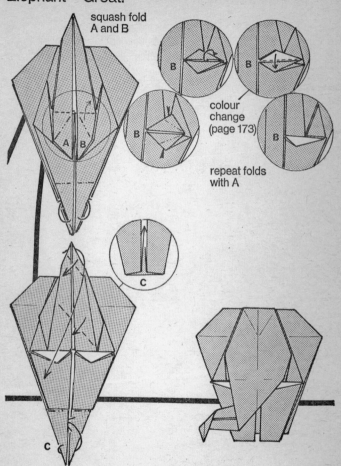

squash fold
A and B

colour
change
(page 173)

repeat folds
with A

Girl in a Mini   Anthony Leaver   England

use a 20 cm square
begin with a preliminary
base
(page 9)
sink point(page 15)

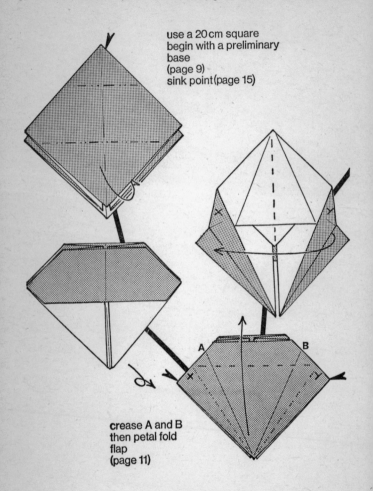

crease A and B
then petal fold
flap
(page 11)

122

Girl in a Mini continued

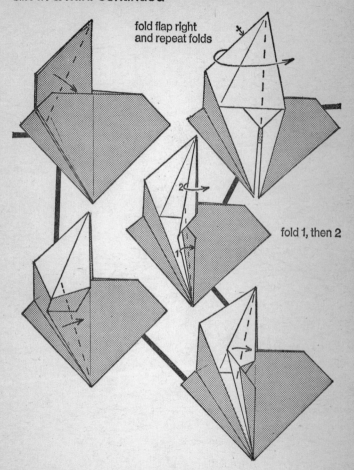

fold flap right
and repeat folds

fold 1, then 2

Girl in a Mini   Such a clever Fold

so

open out

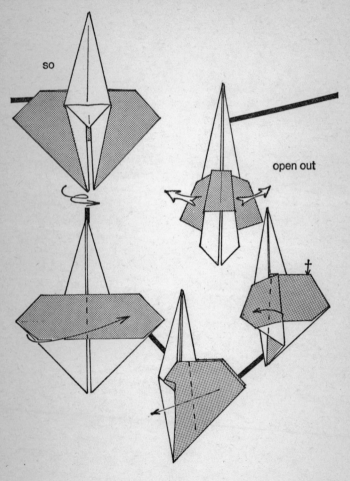

Girl in a Mini   Nearly there

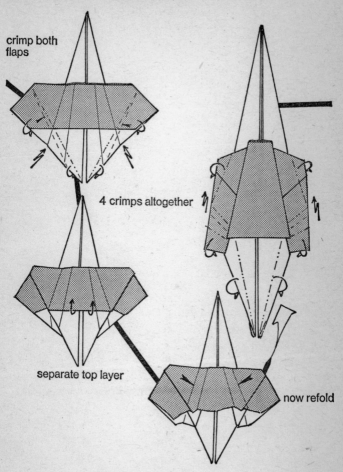

crimp both flaps

4 crimps altogether

separate top layer

now refold

Girl in a Mini   Draw hair and face

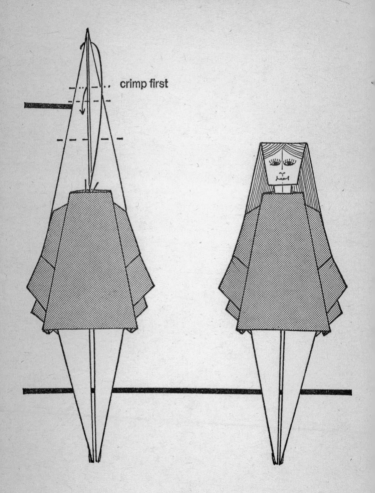

crimp first

Six Point Star

Lewis Simon   America

fold a square in half
fold single layer as
shown

an equilateral
triangle cut

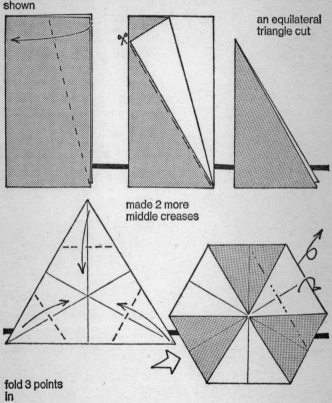

made 2 more
middle creases

fold 3 points
in

Very Attractive Most Ingenious

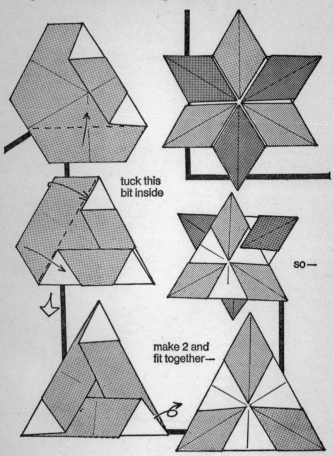

tuck this bit inside

so—

make 2 and fit together—

Fruit Bowl

Alice Gray   America

use a 2 x 3 rectangle

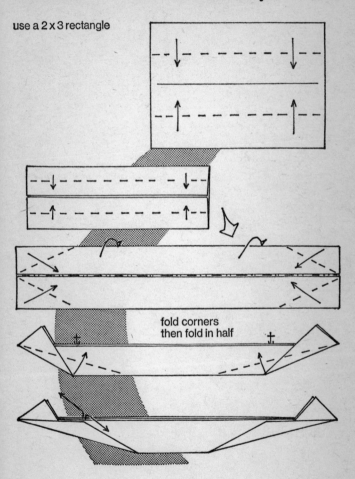

fold corners
then fold in half

Fruit Bowl continued

grip firmly
turn inside out
(remember the Sampan)

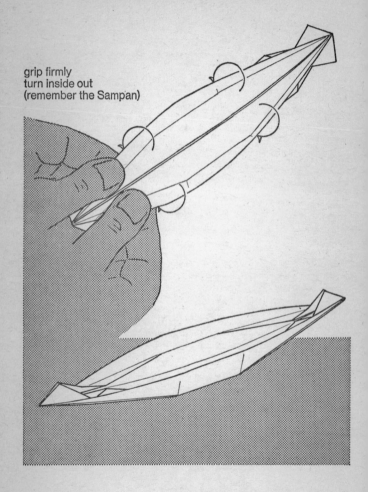

Box in One

Robert Harbin

crease a square
8 times each way

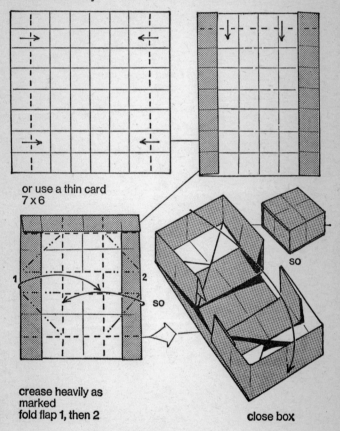

or use a thin card
7 × 6

crease heavily as
marked
fold flap 1, then 2

so

so

close box

Bird

Ligia Montoga   Argentina

cut from a 2 x 1 rectangle
this diamond shape

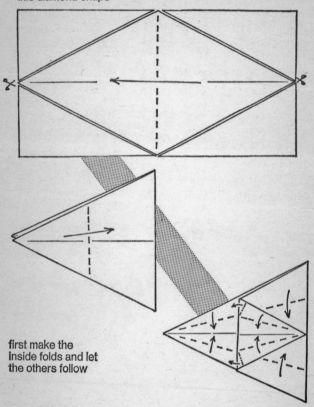

first make the
inside folds and let
the others follow

Bird continued

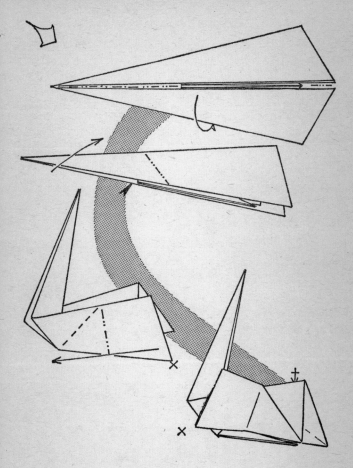

Bird Perfect

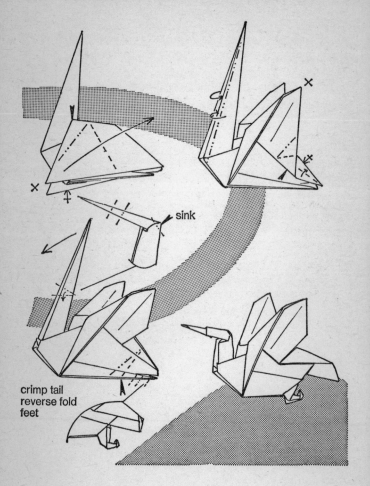

sink

crimp tail
reverse fold
feet

134

Star of David

Fred Rohm America

crease a square into
eighths vertically,
cut off one sixteenth
from each edge

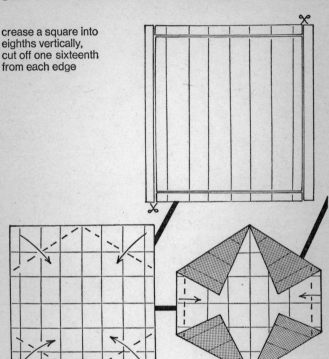

crease the smaller square
into sixths horizontally,
now fold with extreme
accuracy

135

A Genius this man

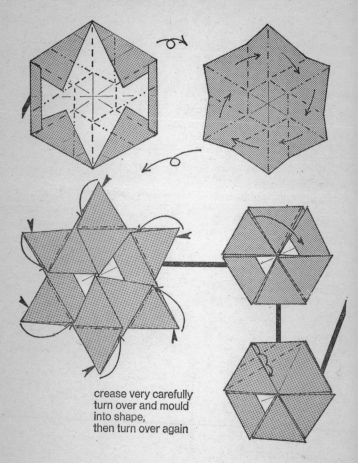

crease very carefully
turn over and mould
into shape,
then turn over again

Star of David continued

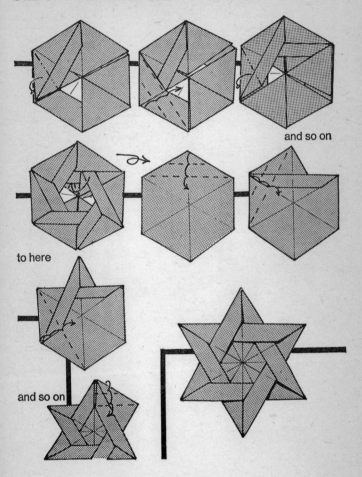

and so on

to here

and so on

137

Dancing Lady

John Smith   Norwich

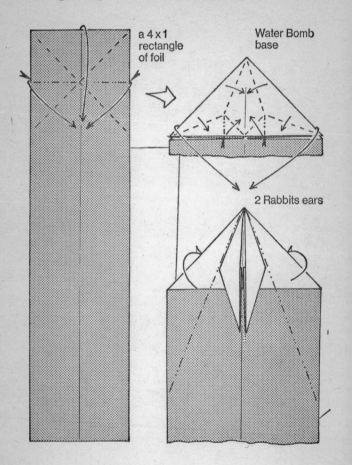

a 4 x 1 rectangle of foil

Water Bomb base

2 Rabbits ears

Classic Original

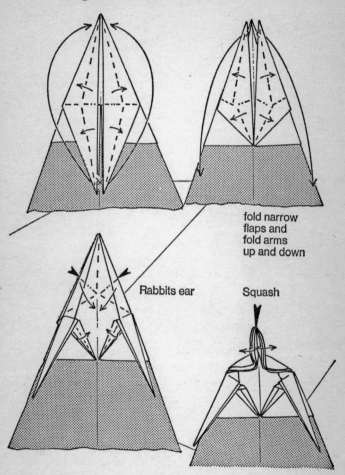

fold narrow
flaps and
fold arms
up and down

Rabbits ear

Squash

139

Dancing Lady continued

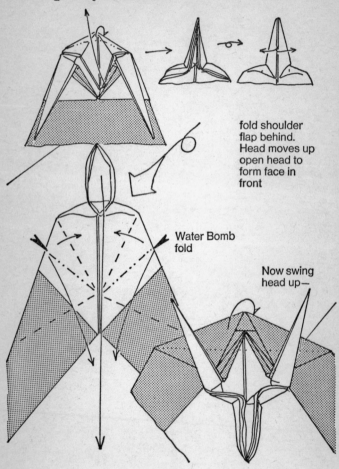

fold shoulder flap behind. Head moves up open head to form face in front

Water Bomb fold

Now swing head up—

140

Dancing Lady continued

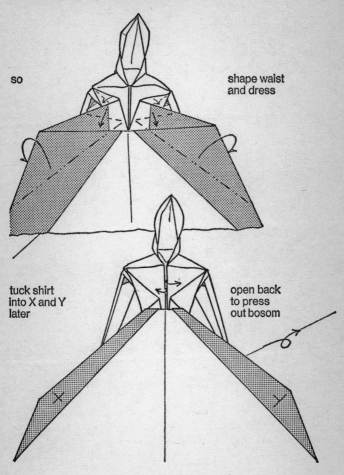

so

shape waist
and dress

tuck shirt
into X and Y
later

open back
to press
out bosom

Dancing Lady continued

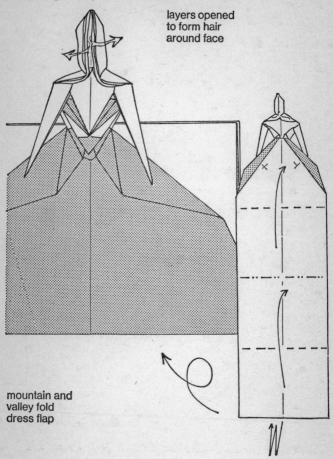

layers opened
to form hair
around face

mountain and
valley fold
dress flap

Dancing Lady continued

dowel fitted into
a base

flap folded to match
dress shape then
tucked into **X** and **Y**
behind

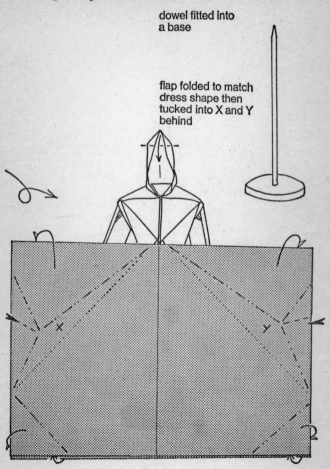

Just blow and She Pirouettes

Santas Christmas Box Robert Harbin England

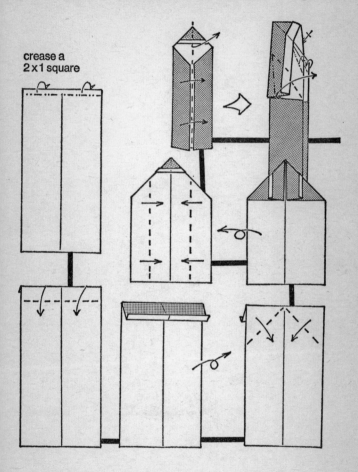

crease a
2 x 1 square

Influenced by Fred Rohm

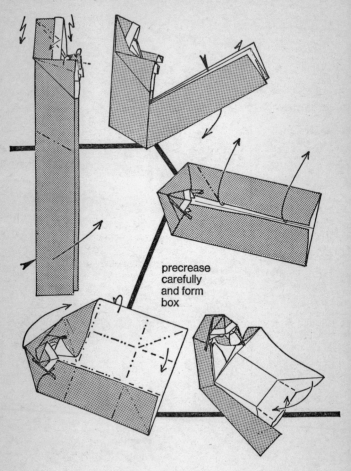

precrease
carefully
and form
box

Santas Christmas Box continued

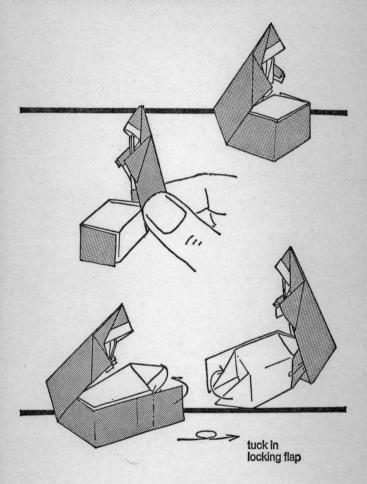

tuck in
locking flap

Turtle   Pat Crawford

crease a square, fold corners
to middle making an inside Blintz

Now treat as a square

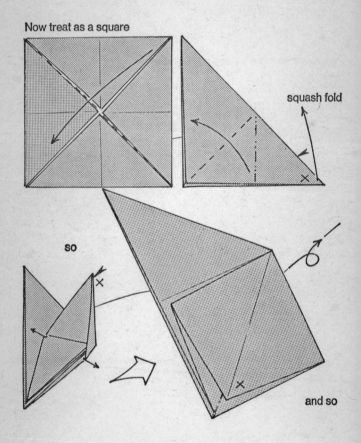

squash fold

so

and so

Turtle continued

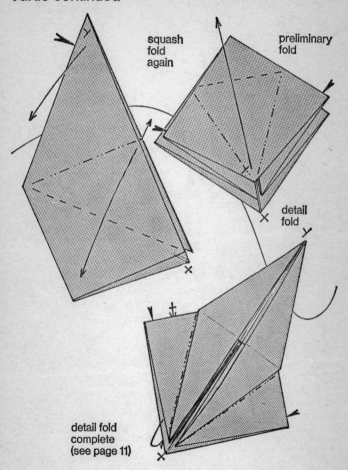

squash fold again

preliminary fold

detail fold

detail fold complete (see page 11)

149

Turtle continued

The Bird Base blintzed inside

hold points and stretch

bring points together

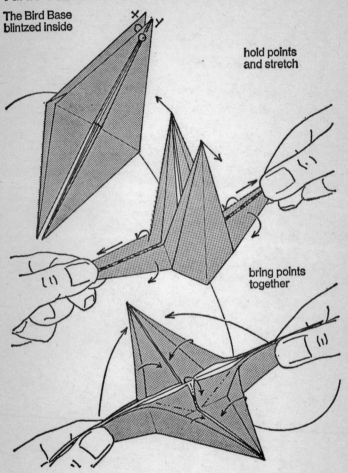

Turtle continued

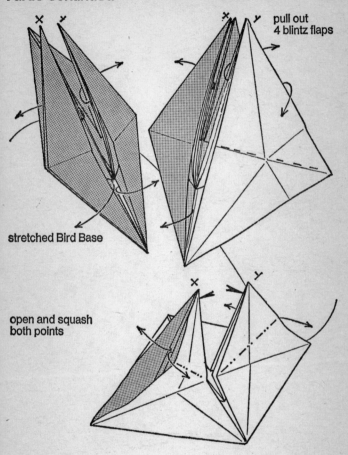

pull out
4 blintz flaps

stretched Bird Base

open and squash
both points

151

Turtle continued

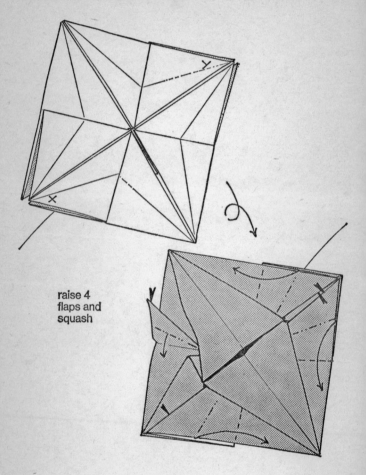

raise 4
flaps and
squash

Turtle continued

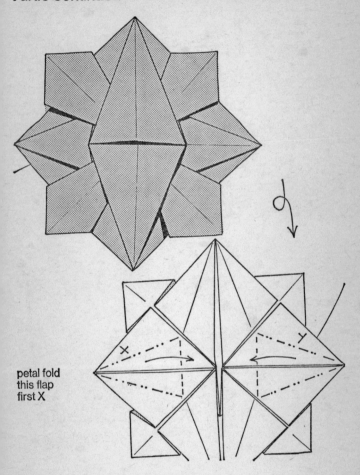

petal fold
this flap
first X

Turtle continued

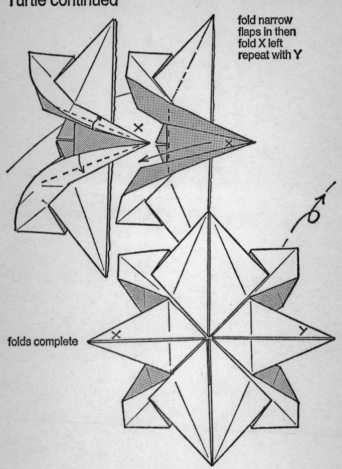

fold narrow
flaps in then
fold X left
repeat with Y

folds complete

154

Turtle continued

note that legs are opposites

from legs
steps 1, 2
3 and 4

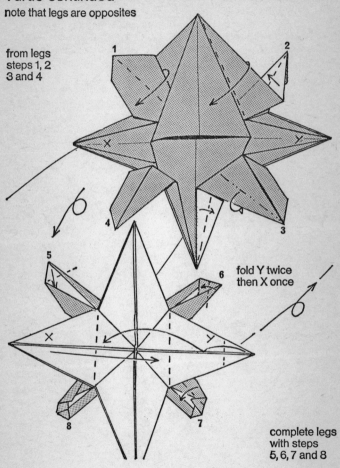

fold Y twice
then X once

complete legs
with steps
5, 6, 7 and 8

Turtle continued

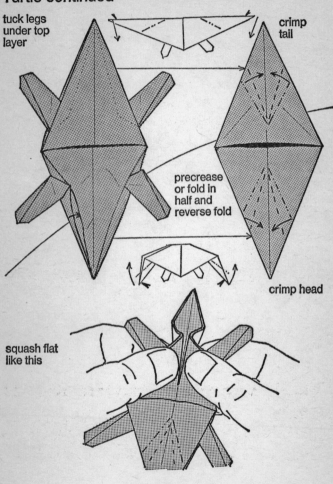

tuck legs
under top
layer

crimp
tail

precrease
or fold in
half and
reverse fold

crimp head

squash flat
like this

3D Head with Tweezers

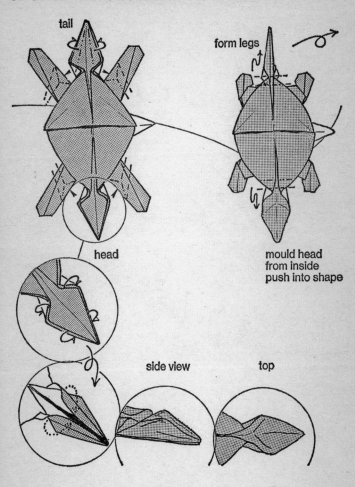

tail

form legs

head

mould head
from inside
push into shape

side view

top

Turtle   A Superb Model

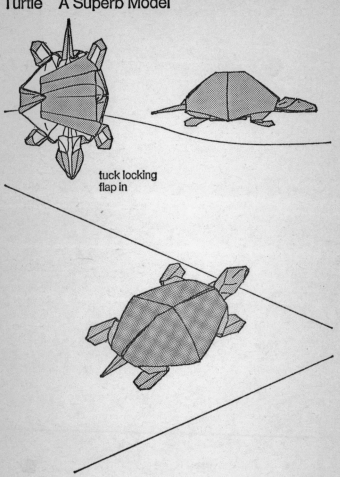

tuck locking
flap in

Flying Pegasus Edward Megrath   Scunthorpe

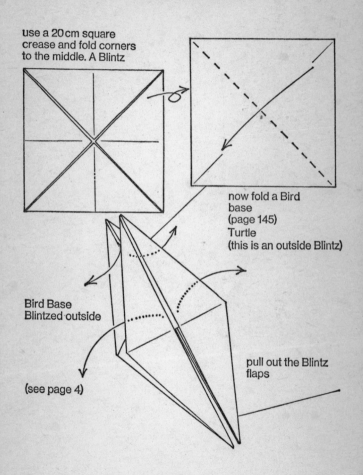

use a 20 cm square
crease and fold corners
to the middle. A Blintz

now fold a Bird
base
(page 145)
Turtle
(this is an outside Blintz)

Bird Base
Blintzed outside

pull out the Blintz
flaps

(see page 4)

Flying Pegasus continued

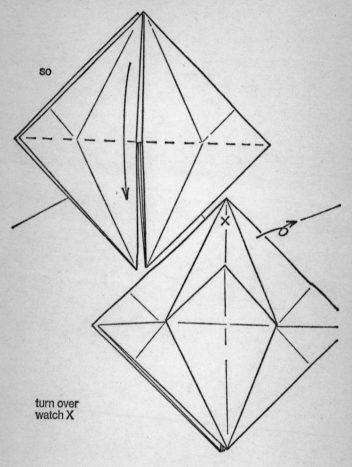

so

turn over
watch X

160

Flying Pegasus continued

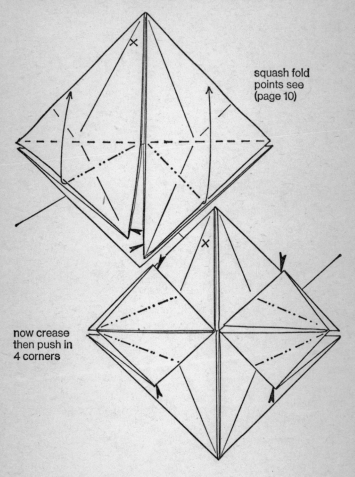

squash fold
points see
(page 10)

now crease
then push in
4 corners

161

Flying Pegasus continued

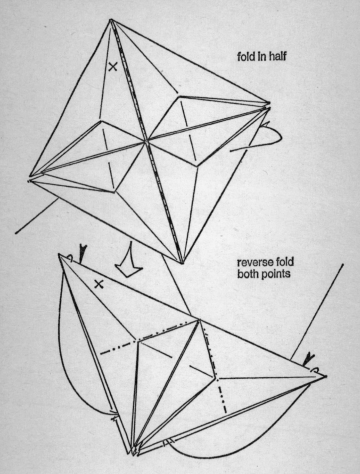

fold in half

reverse fold
both points

Flying Pegasus continued

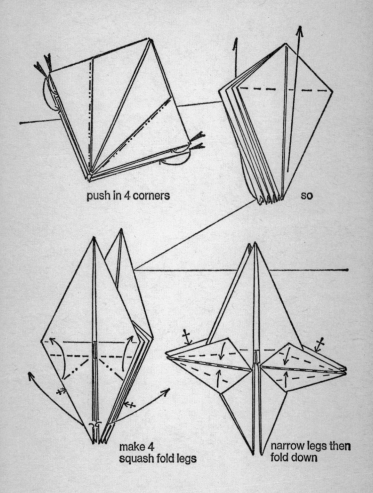

push in 4 corners

so

make 4
squash fold legs

narrow legs then
fold down

Pull legs and Wings flap

reverse fold head and tail

crimp tail

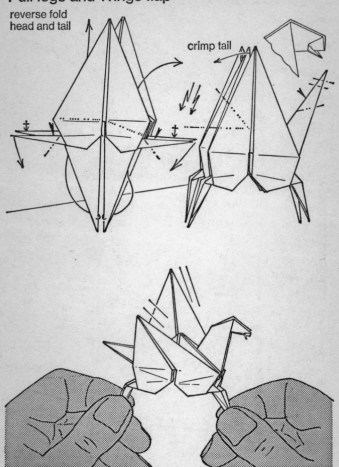

Frog on a Lily Pad   Pat Crawford   America

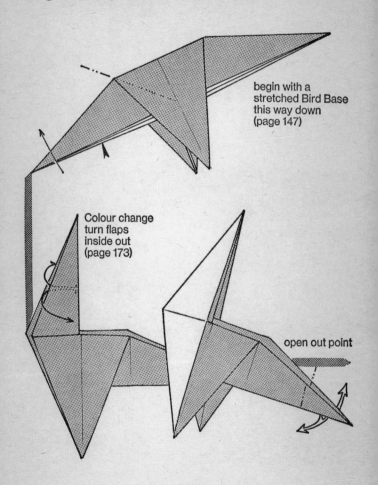

begin with a
stretched Bird Base
this way down
(page 147)

Colour change
turn flaps
inside out
(page 173)

open out point

Frog on a Lily Pad continued

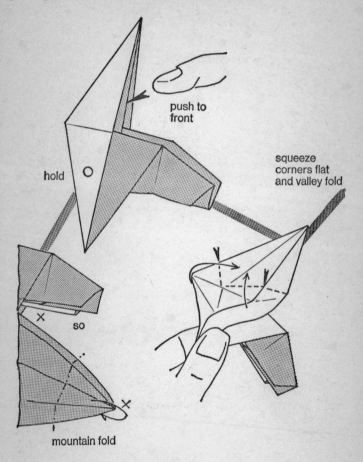

push to front

hold

squeeze corners flat and valley fold

so

mountain fold

Frog on a Lily Pad continued

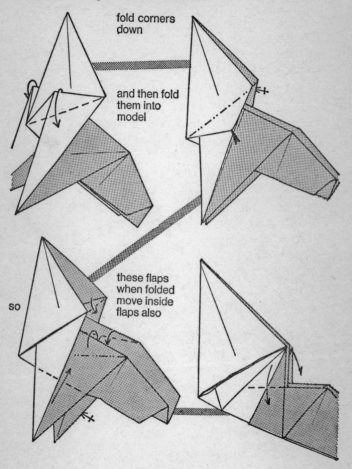

fold corners
down

and then fold
them into
model

these flaps
when folded
move inside
flaps also

so

167

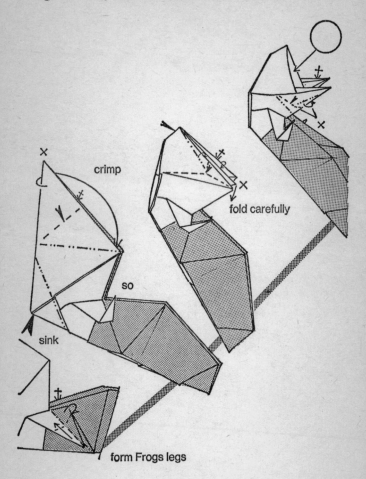

crimp

so

sink

fold carefully

form Frogs legs

A Superb Model

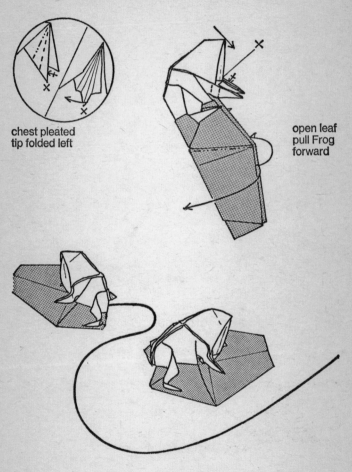

chest pleated
tip folded left

open leaf
pull Frog
forward

Cardinal

Alice Gray   America

begin with a
Bird base
(page 145)
with flaps down

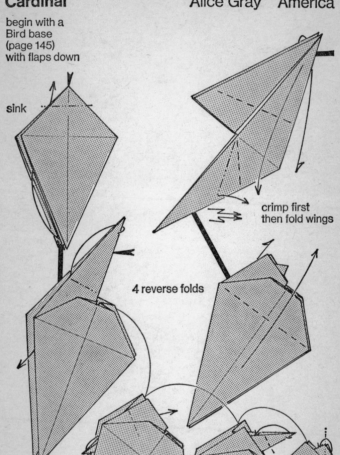

sink

crimp first
then fold wings

4 reverse folds

170

Cardinal continued

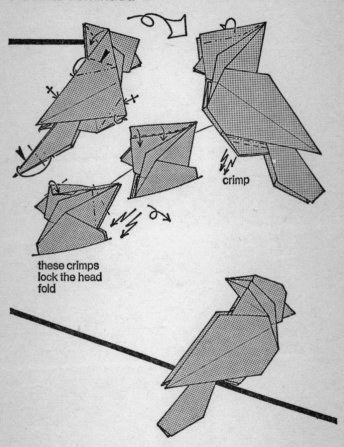

crimp

these crimps
lock the head
fold

Fox   Simon Williams

begin with a stretched Bird Base (page 147)

fold to this point without Blintz folds

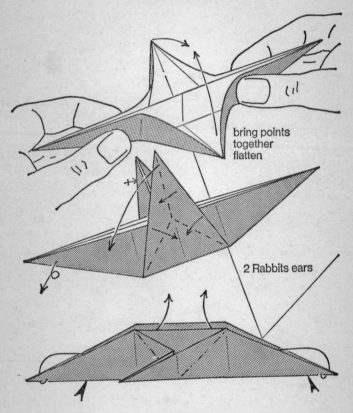

bring points together flatten

2 Rabbits ears

Fox continued

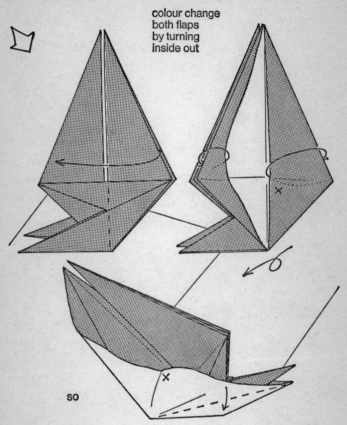

colour change
both flaps
by turning
inside out

so

Fox continued

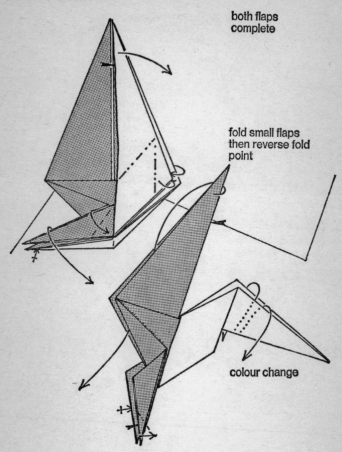

both flaps
complete

fold small flaps
then reverse fold
point

colour change

174

Fox continued

crimp head

crimp tail
one side only

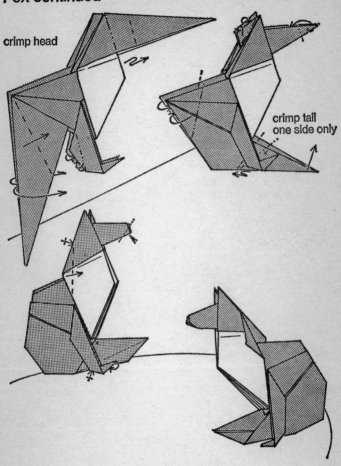

Baby Fox

Toshie Takahama   Japan

half a square
crease middle lines

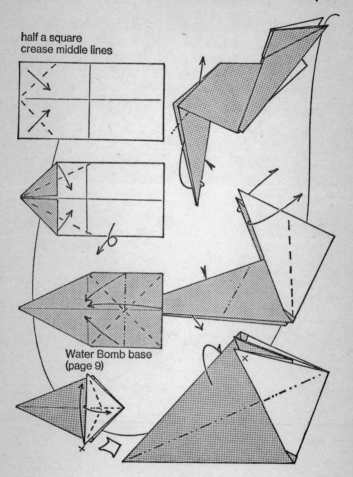

Water Bomb base
(page 9)

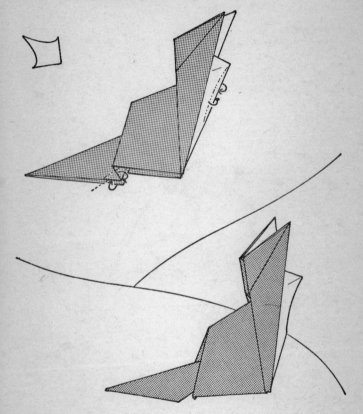

Kangaroo   Sidney French

use a 30 cm square of thin
brown paper. Begin with the
Bird Base (page 145)
without the Blintz

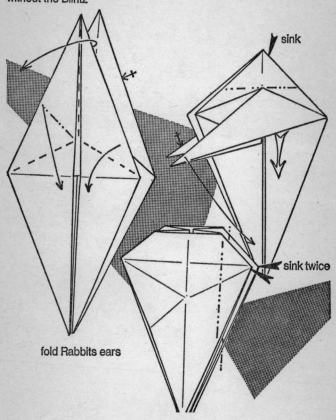

sink

sink twice

fold Rabbits ears

Founder of the British Origami Society

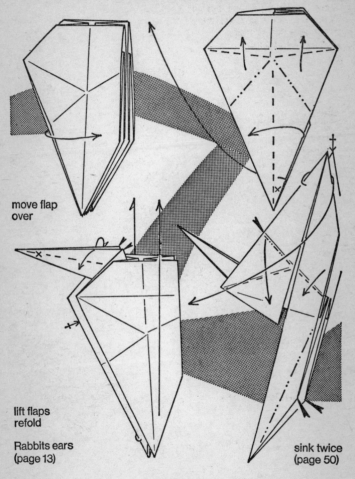

move flap
over

lift flaps
refold

Rabbits ears
(page 13)

sink twice
(page 50)

Kangaroo continued

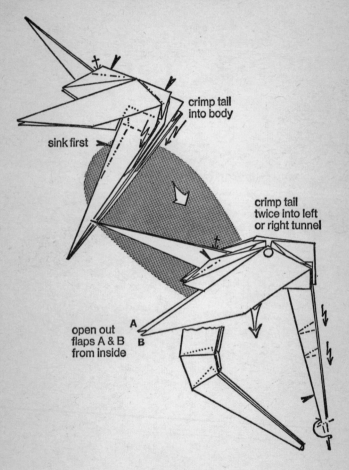

crimp tail
into body

sink first

crimp tail
twice into left
or right tunnel

open out
flaps A & B
from inside

A

B

Kangaroo continued

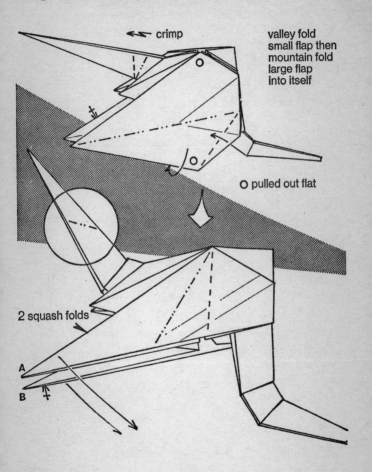

crimp

valley fold
small flap then
mountain fold
large flap
into itself

O pulled out flat

2 squash folds

A

B

Kangaroo   The Head

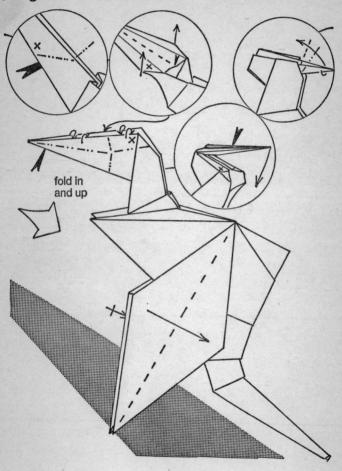

fold in
and up

Kangaroo continued

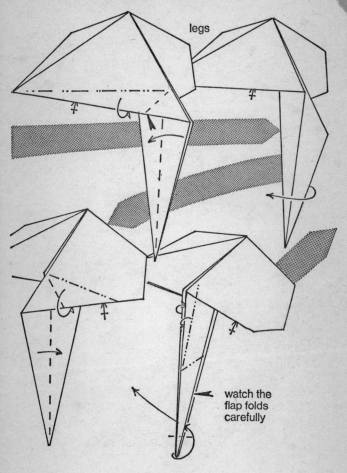

legs

watch the
flap folds
carefully

Kangaroo Magnificent

the forefeet

A

B

The End

BIBLIOGRAPHY

The best Western publications on Origami are those of Harbin, Kenneway and Randlett; the best Japanese works are those of Nakano, Uchiyama and Yoshizawa.

HARBIN, Robert. *Paper Magic*, John Maxfield Limited, 9 The Broadway, Mill Hill London, NW7 3LN, (1971 impression). American edition: Charles Brandford, Newton Center, Massachusetts.
This book, illustrated by Rolf Harris, contains more than one hundred folds and is ideal for the beginner.
— *Origami 1: The Art of Paper-Folding*, The English Universities Press Ltd, London (1968). Hodder Paperbacks, London (1969). American edition: Funk and Wagnalls, New York (1969) (paperback).
Models old and new in pocket format.
— *Origami 2*, Hodder Paperbacks, London (1971).
This sequel to *Origami 1* presents distinguished contributions by contemporary folders along with traditional models.
— *Secrets of Origami*, Oldbourne Press, London (1963). The world's leading folders have contributed original models to this anthology.
KENNEWAY, Eric. *Simple Origami*, Dryad Press, Leicester (1970). Splendid models by the author, with fine contributions by Mooser and Yoshizawa.
— *Origami in Action*, Dryad Press, Leicester (1972).
Models that move, by several folders. Ten little gems.
RANDLETT, Samuel. *The Art of Origami: Paper Folding, Traditional and Modern*, E. P. Dutton & Co., Inc., New York (1961). British edition: Faber and Faber, London (1963).
Fifty-seven models, many of them by the author, along with essays on Origami history, teaching and creation. Jean Randlett's illustrations are superb.
— *The Best of Origami: New Models by Contemporary Folders*, E. P. Dutton & Co., Inc., New York (1963).
Sixty-seven models by fourteen of the world's leading folders, with illustrations by Jean Randlett. This book is an absolute must. The figures are quite outstanding, and the material cannot be found elsewhere. Highly recommended.
— *The Flapping Bird: An Origami Monthly*. Published at $6.00 a year by Jay Marshall, 5082 N. Lincoln Ave., Chicago, Illinois 60625.
New works by the finest creative folders.
NAKANO, Dokuohtei. *Correspondence Course of Origami*, Dokuohtei Nakano Origami Institute, 32-6, Kamikitazawa 3-chome, Setagaya-ku, Tokyo, 156, Japan (1970).
Some 250 original animals, birds, insects, reptiles and human figures of high quality are developed with great technical power from his system of basic folds. The course is in English and is beautifully drawn; finished models, photographs and paper are included. Strongly recommended as a worthwhile investment.

UCHIYAMA, Koshio. *Origami*, Kokudosha, Takata Toyokawa Cho, Bunkyo-ku, Tokyo, Japan (1962).

A major work, concerned in part with cut-and-fold Origami; there are many fine uncut models. Mr Uchiyama's chart of the fundamental crease-patterns in basic folds repays study.

— *Origami Asobi* (Origami Play), Kokudosha, Takata Toyokawa Cho, Bunkyo-ku, Tokyo, Japan (1967).

Twenty-seven imaginative figures by the author.

YOSHIZAWA, Akira. *Origami Dokuhon I* (Creative Origami), Kamakura Shobo Co., Ltd., 21 Ichigaya-Sanaicho, Shinjuku-ku, Tokyo, Japan (1967).

This masterpiece is now published in a larger format, with an English translation included. There are over sixty superlative models, each of which shows the author's genius. Mr Yoshizawa has produced several other beautiful Origami books, including *Origami Ahon and Origami Tanoshi*, which may be ordered directly from Akira Yoshizawa, International Origami Center, P.O. Box 3, Ogikubo, Tokyo, Japan.

CERCEDA, Adolfo. *Folding Money* (Volume 1) Magic, Inc., 5082 N. Lincoln Ave., Chicago, Illinois 60625 (1963).

Eight dollar-bill folds explained by the eminent Argentine folder.

HONDA, Isao. *The World of Origami* Japan Publications Trading Co., 1255 Howard Street, San Francisco, California 94103 (1965).

In this general summary of the editor's previous compilations, the Japanese tradition is presented along with coarsened versions of models by Akira Yoshizawa.

KASAHARA, Kunihiko. *Creative Origami*, Japan Publications Inc., Tokyo; distributed by Japan Publications Trading Co., 1255 Howard Street, San Francisco, California 94103 (1968).

Over one hundred figures, mostly in close imitation of Yoshizawa.

LEWIS, Shari, and OPPENHEIMER, Lillian. *Folding Paper Puppets; Folding Paper Toys*, Stein and Day, New York, Puppets (1962), Toys (1963). *Folding Paper Masks*, E. P. Dutton & Co., Inc., New York (1965).

Three well-illustrated books of simple models.

SAKODA, James Minoru. *Modern Origami*, Simon and Schuster, New York (1969).

Over fifty new models in the author's highly individual style.

TAKAHAMA, Toshie. *Creative Life With Creative Origami*, Makō-sha Publishing Co., Ltd., 14–6, Hongo 4-chome, Bunkyo-ku, Tokyo, Japan. Worthwhile figures of medium difficulty, beautifully illustrated. (Toshie Takahama is the leader of a group of folders in Tokyo. Her address is 24–1, Matsunoki 3-chome, Suginami-ku, Tokyo.)

VAN BREDA, Aart. *Paper Folding and Modelling*, Faber and Faber, London (1965).

Good simple models.

These and other books on Origami can be obtained from:

Magic, Inc., 5082 N. Lincoln Ave., Chicago, Illinois 60625, U.S.A.

The Origami Center, 71 West 11th Street, New York 10011.

John Maxfield Ltd., 9 The Broadway, Mill Hill, London NW7 3LN.

See Robert Harbin's *Secrets of Origami* for a more comprehensive bibliography.